BURBAGE · BETTERTON · FORREST · MACREADY · SALVINI · FORBES-ROBER... · BARRYMORE · GIELG...

GARRICK · KEMBLE · KEAN

BOOTH · FECHTER · IRVING

...SON·SOTHERN·HAMPDEN

EVANS · BURTON

THE
HAMLETS
OF THE
THEATRE

THE
HAMLETS
OF THE
THEATRE

by WILLIAM ACKERMAN BUELL

Foreword by OTIS SKINNER   Introduction by HOWARD LINDSAY

AN OBOLENSKY BOOK

ASTOR-HONOR, INC.
New York, N. Y.

TO
EDWIN BOOTH
in whose memory
The Players live

Author's Publication Preface

The manuscript for this work was completed in 1940, and it was the intention of a distinguished university press to publish. The plan was dropped a few weeks later when the lights began going out in Europe. Otis Skinner was generous enough to do the foreword included in this volume. Howard Lindsay has been most kind to do another. My own introduction stands as I wrote it. Viewed through the arches of the years, it still seems to me to be correct. Certainly the contribution of Otis Skinner, my old friend, and of Howard Lindsay, who recently retired from the presidency of The Players, requires no apologia.

Foreword

No other Shakespearean character has found so many interpreters as Hamlet. Actors of every age, dimension and variety of temperament have exhibited their abilities in the part. It has been given its fantastic touch, its deep purple gloom, as a picturesque, lyric and romantic figure, as a study in psychoanalysis, wholly mad and, again, mentally sound and resourceful. He has been as fat as Falstaff and as meager as Romeo's Apothecary; he has been of every age and every color and complexion; age has not been able to "wither nor custom stale his infinite variety." He has been a student and a lunatic, a hero and a lachrymose villain; he has been portrayed in every civilized tongue. Scholars, poets, philosophers and scientists have striven to solve his paradox, and actors have groped their way after their findings, but Hamlet remains more than a man; he is an "undiscovered country."

It has always been labeled an "actor-proof" part, one that cannot be wholly divested of its interest-commanding value, whether played by an invalid or an athlete. Nearly all the other great characters of Shakespeare must bring something particularly definite and concrete to their interpretation. Lear, Richard, Macbeth, Othello, Iago, Antony, Falstaff, Shylock, Brutus, Caliban, and the vast galaxy that people the plays demand certain positive vocal, mental and physical attributes, even though they present opportunities for a tremendous variant in treatment. Particularly do the young and sentimental parts seem to originate in one special mold, divergent in mood and purpose though they be. But Hamlet stands alone in his universality. Even sex has not proved a bar to its presentation, Sarah Bernhardt, Charlotte Cushman and other actresses having commanded attention in the part and having acquitted themselves with credit.

It has been often said that each of us finds Hamlet in himself. Be that as it may, there are so many dim corners, so many byways and deep abysses in the character that the eternal question mark forever confronts us, and the strife to pluck out the heart of his mystery is endless.

To the actor and the pundit the paradox of Hamlet is distinct in its own way: the former regards him as a vehicle for his emotional and imaginative reactions, which are less impeded by inhibitory breaks than in any other Shakespearean character, and the latter looks to verbal meanings and the psychological origins in his actions. Of course, the more complete the merging of the scholar and the actor the greater the revealing of the soul of Hamlet, but the actor does not pause to analyze during his performance. The more complete his immersion in the emotional stream that carries him on, the more perfect his art. He has never to fight for his opportunities; there are no dull or difficult passages for him to encounter. He does not have to carry the part; the part carries him. His audience is acting his scenes with him; it has commenced to do so even before the curtain has risen on the first act.

In other parts the player may hide behind the bulwark of protective make-up, but even thus armored he may go astray unless he himself is gifted with protean quality. I remember seeing Macbeth played by a noted English actor in London. He was ideal in appearance. I could not conceive a more perfect personification. For some time he held me enraptured, and then—past costume, through wig, beard and paint—came the inevitable revelation of the player's personality, one which by the broadest imagination was far from kin with the Thane of Cawdor. For only five minutes had he been Macbeth.

No actor feels that he has truly written finis to his career until he has shown his mettle as Hamlet, the Dane. Noted comedians have essayed the part. One of America's most popular clowns, George L. Fox, whose "Humpty Dumpty" was the delight of our grandsires, acted Hamlet as the dream of his ambition with his soul keyed to its topmost notch. His audiences laughed at him, but he played it seriously and died content.

OTIS SKINNER

New York City
February, 1940

INTRODUCTION

Any actor who hopes to leave behind him the reputation of having been one of the great actors of his time must play Hamlet. Also, he must play it well enough to earn a high reputation among the judicious of his day. Here, gathered for the first time in one volume, are the contemporary opinions on the performances of all the great Hamlets from the time of Shakespeare to today—from Richard Burbage to Richard Burton. Every student of Hamlet, actor or scholar, will find "Hamlets of the Theatre," by Dr. William A. Buell, required reading.

How much has the style of acting changed in three hundred and fifty years? How did Burbage manage to hold the attention of the restless pit for three hours of Hamlet? How did his concentration survive his seeing the audience as plainly as they saw him? No actor of today would be equal to that!

There have been three major changes, since Shakespeare, in the conditions under which actors play that must have affected the style of their performance. First, moving the theatre indoors and the use of artificial light. Second, withdrawing the performance back off the apron to behind the proscenium arch. Third, the introduction of the box set to replace the wholly artificial setting of wings. Yet so little has been recorded of the changes in acting methods these different conditions must have inspired. I have heard a story about the effect of the introduction of the box set on acting which I shall tell because I think it should be set down in print, and there could be no better place for it than here.

As a young student at The American Academy of Dramatic Arts I had the privilege of hearing Franklin H. Sergeant talk of the genius that was Edwin Booth. Booth is often given credit to this day for founding the modern, natural school of acting and his reputation came about in this way. He learned to act in the day of wings. These were flats on each side of the stage set, parallel to the footlights, to mask off-stage from the audience. They were set far enough apart for the actors to enter between them; i.e., seemingly through the side wall of the set. It would not be surprising if the acting methods were artificial.

In the middle of Booth's career the box set came into use. This introduced for the first time solid side walls giving the set the architecture of a room.

When Booth first found himself acting in a box set, Mr. Sergeant said—in a set with doors, windows and perhaps a fireplace—his sensitivity was so great he knew something different was demanded of him as an actor, something more natural, more quiet, more true. Some of his contemporaries never answered to this demand, and none of those who did meet this challenge met it as well as Booth.

This story has the ring of truth. Certainly the introduction of the box set must have called for something more naturalistic in acting. But how much are we to believe that actors of former days raged and ranted and shouted? Not all of them certainly. The evidence collected for us by Dr. Buell indicates that the highest critical praise was reserved for actors with the quietest methods, starting with Betterton, the second great Hamlet. Colley Cibber wrote of Kynaston, who was born about 1640 and died in 1706, thus being a contemporary of Betterton, as Henry IV, reading the line to Hotspur, "Send us your prisoners or you'll hear of it" in a whisper.

There seems always to have been good actors, bad actors, superior actors and every generation or so, a great actor.

Howard Lindsay

The Players
August, 1966

PREFACE

During the darkest day of the September crisis of 1938, to be relieved with ironic suddenness by the title "Munich Agreement," I found myself in the Victoria and Albert Museum in London searching for pictures of great actors in the role of Hamlet. It is possible that in my dramatic daze I was the calmest man in the capital. When I reported this strange madness to my Oxford tutor, he answered, "Do you know, I think that was wisdom. After all, *Hamlet* goes on." The daze was not a manifestation of the crisis. It had borne me many times the previous summer to the Widener Library at Harvard and to the New York Public Library, and yet again to the Folger Library in Washington. It took me on jaunts to Stratford-on-Avon and to Birmingham, and occupied many hours at the Bodleian Library.

Whence this *Hamlet* lunacy, this pestilential pursuit of the Furies? As a schoolboy, even before the classroom dosage of Shakespeare had been administered, I was enthralled by the Prince of E. H. Sothern and the fair Ophelia of Julia Marlowe. Though my academic instruction in *Hamlet* fell somewhat short of inspiration, my debt to my teacher is great by virtue of one deed. He arranged to have his class journey to Boston to see the most celebrated Hamlet of the day. Sir Johnston Forbes-Robertson's sixty-odd years were not as apparent to us as to some of his critics. Student economy had put us in the balcony. It was enough for us to hear the still matchless voice, and even now I can recall the beauty of the posture of Forbes-Robertson's hands, stretched out toward Ophelia with a tenderness that was eloquent.

Later, as a schoolmaster in the very agreeable company of some sixth formers, I was permitted to study English history with Hamlet left out, but I found him on the stage in Philadelphia in the person of Walter Hampden. Whether there had ever been any reason to doubt it, I was now convinced that Shakespeare had written a great play. John Barrymore made assurance doubly sure. During my college days the inebriated antics of Mr. Barrymore in the films had delighted me. I had followed with mounting excitement his rise to the top of his profession in serious drama, and expected the utmost of his Hamlet. I was not disappointed.

From a fellow member of my profession I have it that the best explanation of the Hamlet mystery was offered by one of his pupils: "The trouble with Hamlet was that he was always letting his self-control get the better of him." Would that my days with *Hamlet* in the classroom might have added one such pearl to the endless string of criticism that has attached itself to the play.

Once when I had turned up yet again at my old school, I discovered unscheduled opportunities for stage productions. The chapel's beautiful gothic cloister with a terrace of green before it pointed a steady finger at Act V, Scene 1. Under a benevolent academic sufferance a group of fourth and fifth formers elected *Hamlet* for their spring term English course, capping the semester with a performance of this scene on the eve of Prize Day. They graciously survived my readings and adumbrations at special 9 P.M. sessions, took notes, learned their lines, and rehearsed. We insured our production against rain and felt that we had acted wisely as we sought shelter for the dress rehearsal. The wisps of fog that hovered about us the next night enhanced the setting like the fulfillment of a producer's dream. Add to this a dim glow of light through the chapel windows and the subdued rumble of the organ, and what more could one wish for? It was an inspired performance. I cherish the statement of the Hamlet of that night, who told me later that of all his school experiences he prized that one the most.

The pursuit of *Hamlet* drove me to the Boston Opera House for Leslie Howard's production one night and put me on a Pullman for New York to attend John Gielgud's the next. I have fallen an easy victim to repeated performances of the Hamlet of Maurice Evans. One thing I chiefly remember of the *Hamlet* in modern dress of Basil Sidney and Mary Ellis is the speech to the players. Not long ago this memory brought me into enthusiastic agreement with John Mason Brown. To my criticism of the reading of a certain actor he replied, "Do you know who among all Hamlets has read that speech right? Basil Sydney!"

In a rash and unguarded moment I asked the obliging librarian at The Players for a book. I should never have done so, for in my ignorance I made a request for a book that did not exist. With startling rapidity that obliging librarian laid a burden upon me. It has not been a weary load to put together a book that would show pictures of actors and sets of *Hamlet* to the extent they might be available. There will surely be a justifiable cry over the choice of actors. The inclusion of some will amaze, and the omission of others enrage. Righteous indignation is another form of personal pleasure. Let the scholars show their learning, and the caustic critics their wit. Under no glare of academic honor do I set up my work, but in the easy expectation of any sort of sling and arrow. This book contains no new theories of Hamlet's madness, nor does it even attempt to evolve a formula for the future actor as to how Hamlet should be played.

Stevenson's delightful remark about an author in his preface occurs to me. He is like an architect strutting briefly with his plans in the portico of a new building. At the conclusion of the author's preface to his first published essays Stevenson wrote, referring to his companion to whom the work had been dedicated, "He, at least, will become my reader."

St. George's School
Newport, R. I.
April 23, 1940

CONTENTS

LIST OF ILLUSTRATIONS

I

THE FIRST LEAP INTO THE GRAVE

Richard Burbage
c. 1567-1619

QUEEN ELIZABETH I died in 1603. The year before, actor-manager Shakespeare produced in his Globe Theatre his *Tragedy of Hamlet Prince of Denmark,* destined to become the most famous play in the English language. Richard Burbage, then in his thirty-fifth year, had already come into his own as the chief player of Shakespeare's company of actors, and his Hamlet added new luster to the favor with which he was held by the patrons of the Globe. Known as "King Dick" for his exciting interpretation of the role of Richard III, Burbage, like his successors, found in Hamlet a part above all others for the display of his talents.

And that is how it all began. Imagination compels one to seek superlatives, for there was a consummation devoutly to be wished. Shakespeare wrote *Hamlet,* Burbage played it, and an adoring audience flocked to see it.

The "pitiful burning of the Globe Playhouse" on June 29, 1613, may have destroyed much priceless evidence to establish the facts not only about Burbage but Shakespeare as well. A small portrait of the head of the actor exists, together with another painted by him. They hang in the gallery of Dulwich College in the southwest suburbs of London.

Burbage played Hamlet as Shakespeare wished him played; that we can safely assume, for the author was present and acted the part of the Ghost himself. The fullest account of Burbage's art, little more than a tribute to a very accomplished actor, was written by Richard Flecknoe, who could never have seen him on the stage. He was not fat because the author wrote "fat and scant of breath." "Fat" meant "sweaty." Like many another player of

1

Richard Burbage
From a painting in the Dulwich College Library

the role, Burbage was not of great stature, but we are no longer bound by a spurious insistence that the stage's "fattest" part was also created for a fat actor.

It is not difficult to conjure up the nature of these first *Hamlet* performances. We have the text of the play, and we know from contemporary prints pretty much what the Elizabethan theatres were like. The "apron" of the stage, minus proscenium arch and curtain, brought the actor into intimate contact with his audience, which stood or sat on benches in somewhat informal array. They were the "groundlings," whose ears Shakespeare accused the ranting actor of splitting. In soliloquy Hamlet took his hearers into his confidence. The inner stage would have been the place for the Queen's closet—the scene between Hamlet and his mother. It undoubtedly contained a bed. (There also must necessarily have been a bed in the final scene of *Othello*.) But scenery and lighting effects as we conceive them today were in the lines spoken by the actors.

No women appeared among the members of the acting companies, nor did they frequent the theatres to any extent. In a very special sense it was a modern-dress *Hamlet,* for the actors wore the garb of their day. Yet the reference to the "customary suits of solemn black" was very likely made consistent, and the same applied to the Ghost "clad in complete steel." Beards were the fashion in the days of Queen Elizabeth and King James. Burbage wore one, for it made sense for Hamlet to say, "Who calls me villain . . . plucks off my beard and blows it in my face?" Swords and rapiers were as much a part of the dress as tie-clasps and belts are today. When Burbage as Hamlet commanded his actors who were playing Horatio and Marcellus to swear "upon my sword," surely a trapdoor had made the "cellarage" available to the Ghost, whose sepulchral "Swear!" was followed by an effective, "Well said, old mole! Cans't work i' the earth so fast?" Ophelia's grave was below the level of the stage platform in order for the mourners to "lay her in the earth," and as often as Burbage acted the part of the Danish prince he leaped into it to struggle with Laertes.

Though surviving bits of evidence attesting to Burbage's talents are meager, they possess a certain antique flavor. They have been published in the works of that overzealous Shakespearean idolater, J. Payne Collier, and some remain unsubstantiated.

> Excellency in the meanest things deserves remembrance; Richard Burbage, and Edward Allen, two such actors as no age must ever look to see again.
> Sir Richard Baker (1568-1645): *Chronicles of England*

And this critique that would do any present-day actor proud:

> He was a delightful Proteus, so wholly transforming himself into his parts, and putting himself off with his cloaths, as he never (not so much as in the trying-house) assumed himself again, until the play was done. He had all the parts of any excellent orator, animating his words with speaking, and speech with action; his auditors being never more delighted than when he spoke, nor more sorry than when he held his peace; yet even then he was an excellent actor still; never failing in his part when he was done speaking, but with his looks and gestures maintaining it still to the height.
>
> Richard Flecknoe: (1664): *Short Discourse of the English Stage*

From a seventeenth-century manuscript in the library of Sir Matthew Wilson of Eshton Hall, Yorkshire, Collier quotes a portion of "A Sonnet on the Pitiful Burning of the Globe Playhouse in London." He supplies the information that Henry Condy is Henry Cundall, joint editor with Heminge of the folio of 1623:

> Out run the knights, out run the lords
>   And there was great ado;
> Some lost their hats, and some their swords,
> Then out run Burbage too;
> The reprobates, though drunk on Monday,
> Pray'd for the Fool and Henry Condy!

From a manuscript in the library of Earl Spencer at Althrop, Northampton, Collier finds an interesting reference. There is no doubt that Burbage is alluded to in the following quotation from "Ratsey's Ghost," a tract without date, but published four or five years after the production of *Hamlet*. Ratsey is addressing himself to the leading actor in a country association:

> And for you, sirrah, (says he to the cheefest of them) thou hast a good presence upon a stage; methinks thou darkenest thy merit by playing in the country; get thee to London, for *if one man were dead,* they will have much need for such as thou art. There would be none in my opinion, fitter than thyself to play his parts: my conceit is such of thee, that I durst all the money in my purse on thy head *to play Hamlet with him,* for a wager.

Scholars, close your eyes. Here follow two undocumented Collier citations, but they are too good to miss:

> If Rossius Richard foames and fumes,
> The globe shall have but empty roomes,
> If thou doest act; and Willes newe playe
> Shall be rehearst some other daye.
> Consent then, Nedde; doe us this grace:

4

Thou cannot faile in aine case;
For in the triall, come what maye,
All sides shall brave Ned Allin saye.

De Burbagio et Reginâ

Hung be the heavens with black, yield day to night!
    Comets importing change shoot through the sky:
Scourge the foul fates that thus afflict our sight!
    Burbage, the player, has vouchsafed to die!
    Therefore, in London is not one eye dry:
The deaths of men who act our Queens and Kings,
Are now more morned than are the real things.
    Queens of the theatre are much more worth,
Drawn to the playhouse by the bawdy scenes,
    To revel in the foulness they call mirth.
    Dick Burbage was their mortal god on earth:
When he expires, lo! all lament the man,
But where's the grief should follow good Queen Ann?

Several manuscripts exist, with slight variations, in praise of Burbage's roles, of which this refers to his Hamlet:

A Funeral Elegy

On ye death of ye famous Actor R. Burbage

Hee's gon, and with him what a world are *dead.*
Oft have I scene him leape into a grave
Suiting ye person (wch hee us'd to have)

Of a mad lover, wth so true an eye,
That there I would have sworne hee meant to dye

(and continuing in modern spelling)

No more young Hamlet, though but scant of breath;
Shall cry "Revenge!" for his dear father's death.

On The Death Of The Famous Actor, Richard Burbage,
who died on Saturday in Lent, the 13th of March, 1618

II

THE RESTORATION HAMLET

Thomas Betterton
c. 1635-1710

THE RETURN OF Charles II in 1660 heralded an era in the English theatre dominated for half a century by Thomas Betterton. His most famous role was Hamlet, which he played almost to his seventieth year. In fact he frequently opened a season as the Prince, with the assurance of rich returns at the box office.

By a certain good fortune the link with Shakespeare had not been broken, for Sir William Davenant, Poet Laureate, playwright and manager, had seen Joseph Taylor play the part. Taylor, who had been coached in the role by Shakespeare himself, acted Hamlet in Burbage's day, and Betterton made his debut in 1661, at the age of twenty-six under Davenant's direction. The Ophelia, a Mrs. Sanderson, probably the first woman to choose acting as a career, became his wife. Like the Garricks of a generation to follow, the Bettertons were noted as a devoted couple.

What record have we of Betterton as Hamlet? There are three entries in the Diary of Samuel Pepys, who saw Betterton's Hamlet at the very first. Each is a glowing tribute to him as the Prince of Denmark from a chronicler who was a caustic critic of plays and players:

> To the Opera, and there saw Hamlet, Prince of Denmark, done with scenes very well, but above all, Betterton did the prince's part beyond imagination.
>
> August 24, 1661.

*　　*　　*　　*

> To the Duke's house, and there saw Hamlet done, giving us fresh reason never to think enough of Betterton.

*　　*　　*　　*

> May 28, 1663.
> To the Duke of York's playhouse, and there saw Hamlet, which

Thomas Betterton
From the painting by Sir Godfrey Kneller

we have not seen this year before, or more; and mightily pleased with it, but above all with Betterton, the best part, I believe, that ever man acted.

*　　*　　*　　*

The longest account comes, decades later, from the pen of Colley Cibber, himself an actor (to which designation one is compelled to add Poet Laureate, playwright, manager, soldier, autobiographer, and scapegoat of Alexander Pope). He gives particular praise to Betterton's art in rendering the Ghost a figure of awe and terror to the spectators:

> You have seen a Hamlet, perhaps, who, on the first appearance of his father's spirit, has thrown himself into all the straining vociferations requisite to express rage and fury, and the house has thundered with applause, though the misguided actor was all the while (as Shakespeare terms it) tearing a passion into rags. I am the more bold to offer you this particular instance, because the late Mr. Addison, while I sat by him, to see the scene acted, made the same observation; asking me, with some surprise, if I thought Hamlet should be in so violent a passion with the Ghost, which, though it might have astonished, it had not provoked him? For you may observe in this beautiful speech, the passion never rises beyond an almost breathless astonishment, or an impatience, limited by filial reverence, to inquire into the suspected wrongs that may have raised him from the peaceful tomb, and a desire to know what a spirit so seemingly distressed might wish or enjoin a sorrowful son to execute towards his future quiet in the grave. This was the light into which Betterton threw this scene, which he opened with a pause of mute amazement; then rising, slowly, to a solemn trembling voice, he made the ghost equally terrible to the spectator as to himself; and, in the descriptive part of the natural emotions which the ghastly vision gave him, the boldness of his expostulation was still governed by decency, manly, but not braving; his voice never rising into that seeming outrage, or wild defiance of what he naturally revered. But, alas! to preserve this medium between mouthing and meaning too little, to keep the attention more pleasingly awake, by a tempered spirit, than mere vehemence of voice, is of all the master strokes of an actor, the most difficult to reach. In this none yet have equalled Betterton.

*　　*　　*　　*

> I never heard a line in tragedy come from Betterton, wherein, my judgement, my ear, and my imagination were not fully satisfied; which, since his time I cannot equally say of any one actor whatsoever. Betterton had a voice . . . which gave more spirit to terror, than to the softer passions; of more strength than melody. . . . The person of this excellent actor was suitable to his voice, more manly than sweet, not exceeding the middle stature, inclining to the corpulent; of a serious and penetrating aspect; his limbs nearer the athletic

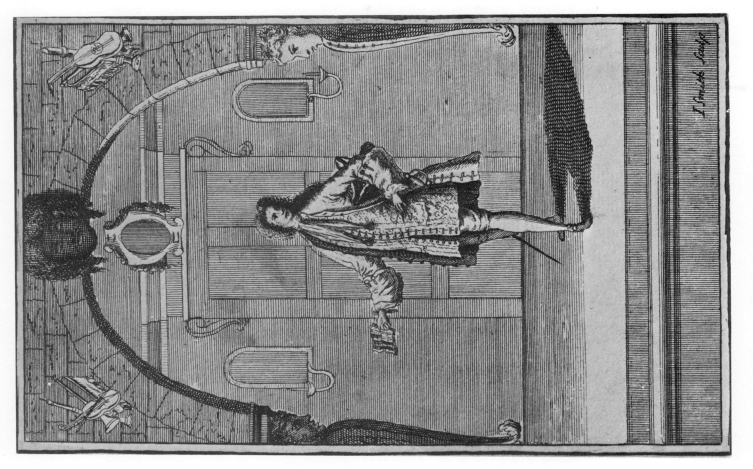

A Hamlet of the Betterton Period

than the delicate proportion; yet, however formed, there arose from the harmony of the whole, a commanding view of majesty, which the fairer faced, or (as Shakespeare calls them) the curled darlings of his time, ever wanted something to be equal masters of.

Apology for His Life (London 1740)

An anonymous, but venomous, attacker of Cibber shared in his praises for Betterton in the Ghost Scene:

> I have lately been told by a gentleman who has frequently seen Mr. Betterton perform this Part of *Hamlet*, that he has observed his countenance (which was naturally ruddy and sanguine) in this Scene of the fourth Act where his Father's Ghost appears, thro' the violent and sudden Emotions of Amazement and Horror, turn instantly on the Sight of his Father's Spirit, as pale as his Neckcloath, when every Article of his Body seem'd to be affected with a Tremor inexpressible; so that, had his Father's Ghost actually arisen before him; he could not have been seized with more real Agonies; and this was felt so strongly by the Audience, that the Blood seemed to shudder in their Veins likewise, and they in some Measure partook of the Astonishment and Horror, with which they saw this excellent Actor affected.

Laureat, (1740, p. 31)

Sir Godfrey Kneller painted Betterton's portrait, which hangs among the treasured canvases in Knole House, Sevenoaks. There is no picture entitled "Betterton as Hamlet," but it is pleasant to rationalize that the illustrators of the period were strongly influenced by what they had seen on the stage. Betterton seems not to have had any particular advantage of physique—he was rather powerful of limb, offset by an uncommanding stature. There is evidence, too, that he had a good voice. The actors did not clothe the character in Elizabethan doublet and hose, but in the court dress of the Restoration—knee-breeches, neck-cloth, curled wig, cocked hat, and all.

Betterton's success as Hamlet is the more impressive when the tastes of the Restoration are considered. The theatres were the toys of royalty, and on their boards flourished the lofty artificialities of the Love and Honor dramas of Dryden along with the vulgarities of the brittle comedies of Congreve and Wycherly. In the light of these preferences, the Hamlet of Betterton must have leaned toward the pompous and ponderous, a style of acting that remained in force until the coming of the dynamic Garrick.

The Continental influences, originally introduced by Inigo Jones, had definitely altered the architecture of the theatre. Performances were now

An interesting variant on the Closet Scene
From the Rowe edition of Shakespeare, published a year before Betterton's death

being viewed through the frame of the proscenium arch. Painted scenery appeared. The Queen's closet got itself out of the inner stage and took on the resemblance of a room with midnight candles and pictures "of two brothers" on the wall.

John Downes established the link with Shakespeare and paid this tribute to the veteran actor:

> The Tragedy of Hamlet; Hamlet being perform'd by Mr. Betterton, Sir William [Davenant] (having seen Mr. Taylor of the Black-Fryars Company act it, who being Instructed by the Author Mr. Shakespeur) taught Mr. Betterton in every Particle of it; which by his exact Performance of it, gain'd him Esteem and Reputation, Superlative to all other Plays . . . No succeeding Tragedy for several years got more Reputation, or Money to the Company than this.

*   *   *   *

> I must not omit praises due to Mr. Betterton, the first and now the only remain of the old Stock, of the company of Sir William Devenant in Lincolns Inn Fields; he like an old Stately Spreading Oak now stands fixt, Environ'd round with brave young Growing, Flourishing Plants: There needs nothing to speak his Fame, more than the following Parts [sixteen are listed, including all the great Shakespearean roles].
> Mr. Dryden a little before his Death in a Prologue, rendring him this PRAISE.
> He like the setting Sun, still shoots a Glimmery Ray, Like Antient ROME Majestic in decay.
> *Roscius Anglicanus or an Historical Review of the Stage* (London 1708)

The first critical edition of the works of Shakespeare by Nicholas Rowe, a later Poet Laureate, appeared just before the death of Betterton, of whom he wrote:

> I cannot leave Hamlet without taking notice of the advantage with which we have seen this masterpiece of Shakespeare distinguish itself upon the stage by Mr. Betterton's fine performance of that part. A man, who though he had no other good qualities, as he has a great many, must have made his way into the esteem of all men of letters, by this only excellency. No man is better acquainted with Shakespeare's manner of expression, and indeed he has studied him so well, and is so much a master of him, that whatever part of his he performs, he does it as if it had been written on purpose for him, and that the author had exactly conceived it as he plays it.
>
> (London 1709)

And finally the young journalist Richard Steele, writing in *The Tatler*, bows before the old actor:

> I was going on in reading my letter, when I was interrupted by

Mr. Greenhat, who has been this evening at the play of *Hamlet*. "Mr. Bickerstaff," said he, "had you been tonight at the play-house, you had seen the force of action in perfection: your admired Mr. Betterton behaved himself so well, that, though now about seventy, he acted youth; and by the prevalent power of proper manner, gesture and voice, appeared through the whole drama a young man of great expectation, vivacity, and enterprise. The soliloquy, where he began the celebrated sentence of 'To be, or not to be;' the expostulation where he explains with his mother in her closet; the noble ardour, after seeing his father's ghost, and his generous distress for the death of Ophelia, are each of them circumstances which dwell strongly upon the minds of the audience, and would certainly affect their behaviour on any parallel occasions in their own lives."

(No. 71. September 22, 1709)

In the manner of his death Betterton exemplified the lofty courage and complete devotion to his art so often the badge of honor of the good player. Approaching seventy-five and in need of funds because of unfortunate investments, he emerged to play yet again before his devoted public. Financially the efforts were successful, but his health was failing. He was billed to play Melantius in *The Maid's Tragedy* of Beaumont and Fletcher. A foot, painfully swollen with the gout, would not receive the necessary slipper. Betterton submitted himself to hot-water treatment, put on the slipper and played his part. But he had been too courageous. A few days later Steele tells us that he went to "see the last office done to a man whom I had always very much admired, and from whose action I had received more strong impressions of what is great and noble in human nature, than from the arguments of the most solid philosophers, or the descriptions of the most charming poets I had ever read."

Betterton's death in 1710 brought him one final, precedent-breaking honor—he became the first actor to be interred in Westminster Abbey, Britain's resting place for her distinguished sons.

The generation following Betterton was a rather arid one as far as a good Hamlet was concerned. There is no evidence in the writings of either Quin or Cibber of any notable Hamlet performance during this period, nor, was there to be one until the emergence of David Garrick.

III

ILLUSTRIOUS PUPIL
OF DR. JOHNSON

David Garrick
c. 1717-1779

ON A CERTAIN DAY in March, 1737, a discontented schoolmaster, accompanied by his ambitious and talented pupil, left the town of Litchfield to seek brighter horizons in London. Samuel Johnson, the master, became the literary arbiter of the capital, and the pupil, David Garrick, the most illustrious actor in the history of the English stage. Garrick's versatility was notable; he played every type of part with astonishing, if not with equal brilliance.

Hamlet may not have been his greatest role, although there is more than sufficient evidence that he was constantly called upon to enact it. There is no one to challenge a claim in his behalf that he was *the* Hamlet of his generation. ("That young man never had his equal as an actor, and he will never have a rival," Alexander Pope declared when Garrick appeared on the London scene.) After first performing the part in Dublin, where the people—with no great originality—honored him with the title of Roscius, he brought *Hamlet* to London on November 16, 1742. It was performed thirteen times that season at Drury Lane out of a total of eighty nights and in opposition to other *Hamlets*. His last performance was given May 30, 1776, during the period of his farewells to his London audiences.

One of the earliest comments on Garrick's interpretation of Hamlet is an unsigned letter in a periodical entitled *The Museum: or the Literary and Historical Register,* dated February 28, 1746.

> He does not in later Tragedies appear to half the Advantage as in Shakespear: probably because our modern Poets abound more in Description and Declamation, and have fewer of those Strokes of

David Garrick
From the painting by Benjamin Wilson

Passion, which are astonishing and yet natural. His action is an excellent comment on Shakespear; and with all the Pains which you have taken with your favourite Author, you don't understand him so well, as if you knew the supplemental Lights which Garrick throws upon him. He sometimes puts me in Mind of what the Wits of the last Age used to say of Betterton . . .; *that he was born to act what Shakespear was born to write:* Yet I fancy there must be a good deal of Difference between them, and though Garrick cannot have so much of that sedate masculine Dignity, yet I question whether even Betterton was so terrible or so moving.

Garrick's immediate popularity brought down a storm of protest from the older actors. It was after witnessing his Hamlet that James Quin exclaimed, "By God, if he is right, we have all been damnably in the wrong!" In the altercation that ensued, Garrick held the upper hand not only in the cleverness of his versified reply but also by his unquestioned success with the public.

"Garrick is a new religion," said Quin. "Whitefield is followed for a time, but they will return to church again."

To which Garrick replied:

> Pope Quin, who damns all churches but his own,
> Complains that heresy infects the town;
> That Whitefield-Garrick has misled the age,
> And taints the sound religion of the stage:
> Schism, he cries, has turned the nation's brain;
> But eyes will open, and to church again!
> Thou great infallible, forbear to roar,
> Thy bulls and errors are revered no more;
> When doctrines meet with gen'ral approbation,
> It is not heresy, but reformation.

Good quarrels were the life blood of the eighteenth-century coffee-houses, and let it be set down for Garrick that he contributed the following kindly epitaph for the monument to Quin in the Abbey Church at Bath:

> That tongue, which set the table on a roar,
> And claimed the public ear, is heard no more
> Closed are those eyes, the harbingers of wit,
> Which spake before the tongue what Shakespeare writ
> Cold is that hand, which, living, was stretched forth
> At Friendship's call, to succour modest worth.
> Here lies James Quin—Deign, reader, to be taught,
> Whate'er thy strength of body, force of thought;
> In Nature's happiest mould, however cast,
> To this complexion thou must come at last.

Garrick possessed most of the physical gifts coveted by an actor with

Garrick in the Closet Scene. Origin Unknown

the possible exception of an inch or two in stature. "Little Davy" was his nickname. Grace in action, springing from an unusually fine figure, an excellent voice, and, in particular, large and expressive eyes seem completely to have fascinated those who saw him.

A little pamphlet of 1755, *The Actor: or A Treatise on the Art of Playing,* maintains that "Mr. Garrick is not handsome," and continues:

> . . . nor did the most enthusiastic admirers of Mrs. Cibber ever call her a beauty, both have features large, strong, and formed for marking the passions; each has the eye piercing in the greatest degree. . . . Mr. Garrick is, perhaps, the most deficient in stature of any man that ever acted an hero, and Mr. Barry looks an unnatural lover for a very short woman; but so perfectly are we reconciled to such trifles in the performances of these great actors, that we never perceive the stature of either to be amiss in the representations.

The comment of a visitor from Germany, one Lichtenberg, written a year before Garrick's retirement, is of special interest. Apparently the actor, in twenty years, had lost none of his vigor:

> He walks and bears himself among the other performers like a man among marionettes . . . His manner of walking, of shrugging his shoulders, of tucking in his arms, of putting on his hat . . . is consequently refreshing to witness. One feels one's self vigorous and elastic, as one sees the vigour and precision of his movements, and how perfectly at ease he seems to be in every muscle of his body. If I mistake not, his compact figure contributes not a little to this effect. His symmetrically formed limbs taper downward from a robust thigh, closing in the neatest foot you can imagine; and in like manner his muscular arm tapers off into a small hand . . . There is a significance and vivacity in his very looks which are catching. When he looks grave, so do we; when he wrinkles his brows, we do so, too; in his quiet chuckle and . . . friendly air there is something so engaging that we rush forward with our whole souls to meet him.
>
> *Vermischte Schriften* (Göttingen, 1844, Vol. III.)

Garrick was great in the dramatic scenes of *Hamlet,* if a trifle in the extreme to satisfy some critics, and possibly too violent toward the Queen and toward Ophelia (Mrs. Garrick did not think Edmund Kean sufficiently so). It was he who introduced the handkerchief "business," whose subsequent adoption by Macready to the annoyance of Forrest had disastrous results at the Astor Place Opera House in New York. Garrick continued the tradition of the overturned chair in the Closet Scene, and to be doubly sure he devised one that would tip over with a clatter as he arose in amazement upon the entrance of the Ghost. But he was too much an artist to employ it with tedious regularity.

Audiences felt his Ghost Scene profoundly moving. Shortly after Garrick's death the actor's biographer, Thomas Davies, wrote:

> When Mr. Garrick first saw the Ghost, the terror he seemed to be impressed with was instantaneously communicated to the audience; his expostulations with the vision, though warm and importunate, were restrained by filial awe. The progress of his impassioned sensation, till the Ghost beckoned him to retire with him, was accompanied with terror and respect. His determination to obey the repeated invitation of the Ghost, by action, to withdraw, was vehemently resolute; his following him awful and tremendous. The approbation of the audience, testified by the loudest applause, was continued till it was interrupted by Hamlet's returning with the Ghost.
> *Memoirs of the Life of David Garrick, Esq.* (London 1780)

The costuming of the part remained more or less conventional at Garrick's hands. He adopted the dress of the French Court, observing the "customary suits of solemn black" of the text. His wig was short, with queue and bag; buckles on the shoes, ruffled wrists and flowing cravat.

Voltaire had roundly attacked Shakespeare for failing to observe the classic rules of good taste in dramatic writing, and under his influence Garrick undertook to improve *Hamlet* by excising the Gravediggers and Osric as being out of key for high tragedy. The experiment was not a success with the public. But the sneering Quin had spoken better than he knew. Garrick's art was revolutionary. The impressive declamation of Betterton gave way to the actor who could project the personalities of his stage characters into the hearts of his hearers.

Garrick's alterations and excisions of the play may appear presumptuous, but people were by no means sure of Shakespeare then. Consider Lord Shaftsbury:

> Our old dramatic poet may witness for our good ear and manly relish. Notwithstanding his natural rudeness, his unpolished style, his antiquated phrase and wit, his want of method and coherence, and his deficiency in almost all the graces and ornaments of this kind of writing; yet by the justness of his moral, the aptness of many of his descriptions, and the plain and natural turn of many of his characters, he pleases his audience, and often gains their ear, without a single bribe from luxury and vice. That Piece of his, which appears to have most affected English hearts, and has, perhaps, been oftenest acted of any which have come to our stage, is almost one continued moral; a series of deep reflections, drawn from one mouth, upon the subject of one single accident and calamity, naturally fitted to move horror and compassion. It may properly be said of this Play, if I mistake not, that it has only *One Character,* or principal part. It contains

Another variant on the Closet Scene
From the works of William Shakespeare, printed by J. Tonson, 1728

no adoration or flattery of the sex; no ranting at the gods; no blustering *Heroism;* nor anything of that curious mixture of *Fierce* and *Tender,* which make the hinge of modern tragedy, and nicely vary it between the points of *Love* and *Honour.*

When Mr. Partridge went to the playhouse in Fielding's *Tom Jones,* it was to see Garrick's Hamlet. The whole account is entertaining to a degree. It is to be found in Chapter V of Book XVI. Charged with cowardice as he beheld the Ghost, Partridge excitedly replied:

> "Nay, you may call me coward if you will; but if that little man there upon the stage is not frightened, I never saw any man frightened in my life." . . . And during the whole speech of the ghost, he sat with his eyes fixed partly on the ghost and partly on Hamlet, and with his mouth open; the same passions which succeeded each other in Hamlet, succeeding likewise in him.
>
> Little more worth remembering occurred during the play, at the end of which Jones asked him, "Which of the players he had liked best?" To this he answered, with some appearance of indignation at the question, "The King, without doubt."
>
> "Indeed, Mr. Partridge," says Mrs. Miller, "you are not of the same opinion with the town; for they are all agreed, that Hamlet is acted by the best player who was ever on the stage."
>
> "He the best player!" cries Partridge, with a contemptuous sneer, "why, I could act as well myself. I am sure, if I had seen a ghost, I should have looked in the very same manner, and done just as he did . . . but, indeed, madam, though I was never at a play in London, yet I have seen acting before in the country; and the King for my money; he speaks all his words distinctly, half as loud again as the other. Anybody may see he is an actor."

Garrick's performances were given in a theatre which had not changed radically. Drury Lane was an ancient building as theatres go, and Covent Garden, constructed in 1731, retained the tiers of boxes, galleries and pit, and stage entrances from the wings with a painted backdrop.

There were bitter rivalries between the Theatres Royal of Covent Garden and Drury Lane. Spranger Barry was possibly a superior Romeo to Garrick, but in what was the longest run for a play up to that time Garrick outran him until the town cried for mercy.

> "Well, what's tonight?" says angry Ned,
> As up from bed he rouses;
> "Romeo again!" he shakes his head:
> "A plague on both your houses!"

The London newspapers of the time gave brief and not very penetrating criticism of performances in the theatre. Particularly noteworthy, therefore, is an essay by a critic who signs himself Hic et Ubique in the *St James' Chronicle* of Saturday, February 22, 1772:

Dramatic Strictures on the Performance of Hamlet

Though it is confessed by the most conversant and oldest attenders upon this performer, that he never played better than he has done in this character, yet let me not be thought ill-natured, if I wished that with the same judgment, skill, and experience, he was some years younger to represent the *young* Hamlet. This fault, if it is one, he cannot amend, and we can only lament.

His entrance upon the stage speaks every circumstance of his situation; but let me differ with great deference to him, about the manner of speaking the speech to his mother. Mr. *G.* in my opinion, takes away from the dignity, solemnity, and manhood of the character, by giving a kind of feminine sorrow to it: The son, though ever so tender, should not sink the prince in his grief: Besides, is his a more confirmed melancholy from the conduct of his mother, than from the immediate bursting of sorrow for his father, who has been dead two months?

But I have that *within* which passeth show—therefore the *inward* not external exhibition of sorrow must be the guide to the actor through the first scene. As no writer in any age penned a ghost like Shakespeare, so, in our time, no actor ever saw a ghost like Garrick. The soliloquy which finishes the Second Act is a master-piece of reasoning and passion—and is a model of this kind of writing—there is no scene of dialogue more interesting or impassioned. May I venture to ask if Mr. Garrick would not please the judicious more, by exerting his powers less, in this soliloquy?

Act III. *To be or not to be*—has not the fault in execution which I hinted at above—the same with Ophelia, if not played with levity, will appear too severe for the character of Hamlet. Shakespeare, by asking the question, *Ha, Ha,* are ye honest? with a laugh, is a direction for the player. It is not natural to think that Hamlet in love with Ophelia would be too rough with her—she has done nothing to deserve it, and it is the best distinction of feigned, from true madness, that he would choose from his feelings to support it with as little outrage as possible to her he loves; of the two ways in his power, he would naturally choose that which would give her and himself the least pain. The advice to the players (never more wanted, and less attended to than at present) is *well spoken, with good accent, and good discretion.* It is a pity that Hamlet is obliged in his rant at Ophelia's grave to contradict himself: If I were Hamlet I would give up the rant and the applause altogether. Mr. *G.* may do as he pleases.

We are now come to the great scene of this wonderful play. It has been matter of much dispute in the newspapers and coffee-houses, whether the two pictures should not be large ones hanging up in the Queen's Closet, rather than miniatures taken out of his pocket. As there was no cessation from playing but in the fanatical

The FOURTH TIME

At the THEATRE ROYAL in DRURY-LANE

This present Wednesday, Feb. 10, 1773

HAMLET.

(With ALTERATIONS.)

Hamlet by Mr. GARRICK,

King by Mr. JEFFERSON,

Ghost by Mr. BRANSBY,

Horatio by Mr. PACKER,

Polonius by Mr. BADDELEY,

Laertes by Mr. J. AICKIN,

Rosencraus Mr. DAVIES, Guildenstern Mr. FAWCETT,

Marcellus Mr. ACKMAN, Player King Mr. KEEN,

Queen by Mrs. HOPKINS,

Player Queen by Mrs. JOHNSTON,

Ophelia by Mrs. SMITH.

To which will be added (Not Acted this Season)

Polly Honeycomb.

Mr. Honeycomb by Mr. PARSONS

Scribble by Mr. DODD,

Ledger by Mr. BRANSBY,

Mrs. Honeycomb by Mrs. JOHNSTON,

Nurse by Mrs. BRADSHAW.

Polly Honeycomb by Miss POPE.

The Comic Opera of The WEDDING RING is obliged to be deferred
on Account of Mr. BANNISTER's Indisposition.

To-morrow, (Not Acted this Season) The CONSCIOUS LOVERS.
To which will be added [The Sixteenth Time] The New Farce of The IRISH WIDOW.
The Widow Brady by Mrs. BARRY.

Playbill. February 10, 1773

times, from Charles the First 'till the Restoration, the manner of performing the scenes in the author's time is undoubtedly handed down to us. Besides has not he taken care to give us a hint that the pictures should be in little? *Those that would make mowes at him while my father lived, give twenty, forty, fifty, an hundred ducats apiece for his picture in little.* A critic who sat near me on the second night of performing this play, and whom I judged, from his discourse, to be an antiquarian, very significantly assured us, that the two pictures should be golden medals in cases, which, he said, would put an end to the dispute, by convincing everybody of the propriety of his thought. This gentleman slept more than half the play. Let me just mention that there was a particular look of that excellent actress, the late Mrs. Pritchard, when Hamlet says—*Do you see nothing there?* which was much wanted. She turned her head slowly round, and with a certain *glare* in her eyes, which looked everywhere, and saw nothing, said,

Nothing at all; yet all that's here I see! which gave an expression and horror to the whole not to be described: That circumstance excepted, I was contented, and expressed my satisfaction as warmly as any gaping spectator of 'em all. As I mean nothing but to search after truth, and to be of as much service as I can to the rising generation of critics and actors (who will always take their favourite for their standard to judge and act by), let me propose a doubt, which Mr. Garrick himself has begot in me. As he must have felt the good effects of a low tremulous manner in many parts of this scene with his mother, would not the whole, executed in the same manner, affect an audience more deeply? I am aware that the actor might urge the great effect of contrast, and that acting, like a picture without light and shade, or a certain variety, would fail in art; it may be so. But could I be as expressive and audible in that under-speaking, as I could in a louder exertion of my powers, I would follow nature wherever she guided me, though the two galleries should fall asleep at the performance! *Dixi!*

Nothing can be said in praise of the remaining parts of the play, notwithstanding that many pearls may be found among the rubbish. If I had my will, I would quit the theatre at the end of the third act, though Roscius himself were to perform the part of Hamlet. It is some comfort to us little beings, that the most sublime genius can sink from heaven below the earth, that our greatest philosopher, Bacon, and our greatest general, Marlborough, could descend to the weaknesses of the lowest minds; and that our greatest poet, Shakespeare, could produce the two last acts of Hamlet.

During Garrick's farewell performances another critic wrote of him in the issue of October 19, 1776:

In this character for 30 years he stood alone. There were some little circumstances, however, which proved this great man to be a mortal. . . . On seeing his father's ghost, which he is prepared to see,

Mr. Garrick throws himself into such an attitude, that if Horatio did not support him, he must fall down. Allowing reasonably for stage trick, this appears to us to be extravagantly overdone; for Hamlet immediately speaks one of the most manly and most determined speeches that could have been made, and which a man knocked down with fear could not have spoken. "Be thou a spirit of health, or goblin damned, etc, I'll speak to thee!"

Throughout his career Garrick belonged to the inner circle of the leaders in the arts and in government. His death in 1779 occurred two and a half years after his retirement, and his burial at Westminster Abbey was an occasion of national solemnity.

The London stage had not long to wait for the appearance of another dominant figure. The interval between Garrick's retirement and the advent of John Philip Kemble's Hamlet was brief indeed.

IV

LIKE A MAN IN ARMOR

John Philip Kemble
c. 1757-1823

TO THE MARRIAGE of Roger Kemble, itinerant player, and Sarah Wood, actress, were born twelve children, two of whom are famous in the annals of the stage and two others well known. The eldest child was the greatest tragic actress of her day, Mrs. Sarah Siddons. The third, George Stephen, was fat. He played Falstaff without artificial padding and was a theatrical manager of considerable success. Oddly enough, he also played Hamlet. Charles, the youngest son, and another player of Hamlet (though dubbed by Macready "a first-rate actor in second-rate parts"), was, with his brilliant daughter, Fanny, a great favorite with American audiences.

"Since brevity is the soul of wit and tediousness the limbs and outward flourishes," we come to John Philip Kemble, the second member of the family.

There is a story to the effect that to outwit their rivals at Drury Lane the managers of Covent Garden dispatched a messenger to secure the services of a talented young Kemble. Alas, the messenger made a faulty identification. Covent Garden got Stephen, and John went to Drury Lane. There he made his first appearance, on September 30, 1783, in the role of Hamlet. Opinions of his interpretation were sharply divided, but one thing is certain. It was original. With the memory of Garrick still green, there were difficult barriers to overcome. Still, for thirty years John Philip Kemble represented the Prince to the high satisfaction of his public.

It may well be that we look next upon the first "first-night notice" of an

BY His MAJESTY's COMPANY

At the Theatre-Royal in Drury-Lane,

This present TUESDAY, Sept. 30, 1783,

HAMLET.

(As originally written by Shakespeare)

Hamlet by Mr. KEMBLE,

(From the Theatre Royal, Dublin; being his first Appearance upon that Stage.)

King by Mr. PACKER,

Horatio by Mr. FARREN,

Polonius by Mr. BADDELEY,

Laertes by Mr. BARRYMORE,

Ostrick by Mr. R. PALMER,

Rosencraus by Mr. PHILLIMORE,

Guildenstern by Mr. WILLIAMES,

Player King by Mr. CHAPLIN,

Marcellus, Mr. WRIGHTEN, Lucianus, Mr. WALDRON,

Gravediggers by Mr. PARSONS & Mr. BURTON,

And the Ghost by Mr. BENSLEY.

Ophelia by Miss FIELD,

Player Queen by Mrs. HEDGES,

And the Queen by Mrs. HOPKINS,

To which will be added

The QUAKER.

Lubin by Mr. SUETT,

Solomon by Mr. PARSONS,

Easy by Mr. WRIGHTEN,

And Steady by Mr. STAUNTON,

Gillian by Miss FIELD,

Cicely by Mrs LOVE,

And Floretta by Mrs. WRIGHTEN.

Places for the Boxes to be taken of Mr. Fosbrook at the stage-Door.

*** The Doors will be opened at HALF after FIVE o'Clock,

To begin at HALF after SIX.   Vivant Rex & Regina.

Playbill. Kemble's London debut, September 30, 1783

Kemble about 1790

actor. The Mr. Henderson referred to in the criticism is John Henderson (1747–1785), an important rival of Garrick and Kemble, known as the "Bath Roscius."

Theatrical Intelligence

Mr. Kemble, from the Theatre Royal, Dublin, last night made his first appearance at Drury-lane Theatre, in Shakespeare's Hamlet. Few are the characters in the drama that require so many requisites to enable a performer to rise above mediocrity, as the one in which this Gentleman chose to make his first *entrée;* and therefore, as he acquitted himself to the general satisfaction of the audience, we doubt not when a little more used to his situation, but he will prove, if not the first, at least equal to any of our present male votaries at the shrine of Melpomone. He possesses an excellent stage figure; a voice that has a variety of tones, in the modulation of which, he appears a complete master; an expressive countenance, and his action is, by no means, confined or extravagant. There is a very great family likeness between him and his sister, Mrs. Siddons; and, like her, he appears to have studied every little nicety that is probable to catch the attention and applause of the audience. To speak of him by comparison—He does not deliver so much from the heart, and to it, as Mr. Henderson; he does not so truly impersonate the character, but his coloring is fashioned with more grace, and his delineations are more articulate and critical. In level speaking he is superior to everyone: In passion, Mr. Henderson and others are superior to him.
The London Chronicle, (October 1, 1783.)

Majestic dignity and scrupulous grace characterized Kemble's stage presence. Hazlitt, who preferred Edmund Kean, said that he played Hamlet "like a man in armor." The portrait by Sir Thomas Lawrence in the National Gallery suggests this. However, let due allowance be made for a slight oversentimentalizing of the subject, with a note that Lord Byron's boxing instructor did some of the posing. Kemble's voice was far from flawless, and a habit of pausing over words annoyed many of his hearers. Yet an essentially sound knowledge of and perseverance in his art brought him to the head of his profession.

In the eyes of a few critics Kemble offended by a costume too elaborate and colorful; but if he gave offense, he also set a style. Hamlet and the characters who appeared with him on stage never again attempted contemporary costume, unless one excepts the recent modern-dress versions. In point of fact the Hamlet garb became more showy, and even gaudy, up to the middle of the nineteenth century—ribbons and orders sprouting in abundance on his chest. One of these decorations that Kemble especially liked, and aroused criticism for wearing, was the Danish Order of the Elephant. It was, of course, an anachronism for an almost legendary Danish

29

John Philip Kemble
From the painting by Sir Thomas Lawrence

An unmistable Kemble; a print dated 1788

The Garrick manner of dress; madness in the hose

prince of the third century to affect a royal badge of honor created at the very earliest in the thirteenth.

Tom Davies, biographer and admirer of Garrick, had the tolerance to speak well of the "new Hamlet":

> Since my remarks on this tragedy went to the press, I have seen a new Hamlet, in the person of Mr. Kemble, brother to Mrs. Siddons. I congratulate the public on the prospect of much rational entertainment, from the joint efforts of two persons of uncommon genius in the art which they profess.
>
> Though in drawing the outline of Hamlet, it was scarcely possible Mr. Kemble should differ from preceding actors, yet his particular emphasis, pauses, and other novelties in acting, have surprised the public and divided the critics; some of whom greatly censure, while others as warmly extol, his peculiarities.
>
> Mr. Kemble's pauses are, I believe, very judicious, though to many they appeared long.
>
> In the impassioned scene between Hamlet and his Mother in the third act, Kemble's emphasis and action, however different from those of all former Hamlets we have seen, bore the genuine marks of solid judgment and exquisite taste. I never saw an audience more deeply affected, or more generously grateful to the actor who had so highly raised their passions.
>
> Mr. Kemble is tall and well made; his countenance expressive, his voice strong and flexible, his action and deportment animated and graceful. His salutations are said by some to be too much studied, and, in the scene of fencing, too formal and ceremonious.
>
> *Dramatic Misc.* (1784)

All critics, however did not approve:

> Behold the macaroni *Prince of Denmark!* Invariably the same, *still life* and *affectation.* When divested of the *tinsel dignity,* created by *singularity,* superiority must recommend him to public notice. Though the reflective power is sometimes beautiful and original, the effect is destroyed by external decoration; the frame being adorned with *pantomimical emblems,* instead of *animated representations* from nature.
>
> *The Green-Room Mirror* (London 1786)

Early nineteenth-century critics appear to have considered Hamlet far from an actor-proof part:

> The Hamlet of Mr. Kemble is certainly the greatest performance of that master, if the difficulty of preserving the interest of such a character be considered. In his hands we neither perceive the length of the play, nor find any leisure to contemplate its absurdity.
>
> *The Stage* (No. 8. - Vol. I January 5, 1815)

In Alexander Chalmers' account of Kemble published in 1838, we must discount somewhat a natural veneration for "the good old days":

The Public are respectfully informed, that Mr. KEMBLE, from the Theatre Royal, Drury Lane, is engaged to perform here Eight Nights.

THEATRE, BIRMINGHAM.

This present THURSDAY, *June* 28, 1798, *will be presented,*

The TRAGEDY of

HAMLET,
PRINCE of DENMARK.

The Part of Hamlet, by Mr. KEMBLE,

Horatio,	Mr. HARLEY,
Laertes,	Mr. M'CREADY,
Ostrick,	Mr. BETTERTON,
King,	Mr. SPARKS,
Polonius	Mr. POWELL.
Rosencraus,	Mr. WHITMORE,
Guildenstern,	Mr. CLAREMONT,
Grave Diggers,	Messrs. LEE and DYKE,
Player King,	Mr. JONES,
Lucianus,	Mr. FOLLETT,
And Ghost,	Mr. RICHARDSON.
Queen,	Mrs. SPARKS,
Player Queen,	Mrs. WHITMORE,
And Ophelia,	Miss LEAK,

(Who has renewed her Engagement for Two Nights.)

DANCING,
By Mr. PLATT and the Miss DENNYS.

To which (by particular Desire) will be added, the FARCE of The

ADOPTED CHILD.

(As performed at the Theatre Royal, Drury-Lane, with universal Applause.)

Michael,	Mr. BETTERTON,	Spruce,		Mr. LEE.
Record,	Mr. POWELL,	Nell,		Mrs. GILBERT,
Lesage,	Mr. RICHARDSON,	Clara,		Mrs. FOLLETT,
Sir Bertrand,	Mr. CLAREMONT,	Lucy,		Mrs. FREDERICK,

And the Adopted Child, Miss SIMS.

The Doors will be opened at Six, and begin precisely at Seven o'Clock.—BOXES, 4s. PIT, 2s. 6d. GALLERY, 1s.
TICKETS for the BOXES and PIT, and PLACES to be taken of Mr. SANDERSON, Box Book-keeper, at the Stage Door, in Queen-Street, every Day from Ten to Two o'Clock.—TICKETS also to be had at Mr. PEARSON's, in the High Street.
Servants, who are to keep Places, are desired to be at the Stage Door a Quarter before Six o'Clock.
Nothing under FULL PRICE can be taken, nor ANY PERSON admitted behind the Scenes.

Second Night of Mr. Kemble's Engagement will be on Friday the 29th instant, when will be presented the Tragedy of *King Richard the Third*; King Richard, Mr. Kemble; to which will be added, the Musical Farce of *No Song, No Supper*; Margaretta, Miss Leak.

William Henry West Betty
Thirteen year old prodigy as Hamlet in 1805

William Henry West Betty
From the painting by J. Northcote, R.A.

Theatre Royal, Drury-Lane.

This present THURSDAY, April 4, 1805.
Their Majesties Servants will act the Tragedy of

HAMLET.

Hamlet by the YOUNG ROSCIUS,

Claudius, *King of Denmark*, Mr. POWELL,
Polonius, Mr. DOWTON,
Laertes, Mr. BARTLEY,
Horatio, Mr. HOLLAND,
Rosencrantz, Mr. LEE,
Guildenstern, Mr. FISHER,
Osrick, Mr. PALMER,
Marcellus, Mr. COOKE, Bernardo, Mr. MALE,
Francisco, Mr. EVANS, Priest, Mr. WEBB, Sailor, Mr. CHATTERLEY,
First Actor, Mr. MADDOCKS, Second Actor, Mr. PURSER,
First Grave-digger, Mr. SUETT,
Second Grave-digger, Mr. GRIMALDI,
Ghost of Hamlet's Father, Mr. WROUGHTON.

Gertrude, *Queen of Denmark*, Mrs. POWELL,
Ophelia, Mrs. H. JOHNSTON,
Actress, Miss TIDSWELL.

To which will be added the Farce of

The LIAR.

Sir James Elliot, Mr. DE CAMP,
Old Wilding, Mr. POWELL,
Young Wilding, Mr. ELLISTON,
Papillion Mr. WEWITZER.

Miss Grantham, Miss, MELLON,
Miss Godfrey, Mrs. SONTLEY, Maid, Miss TIDSWELL.

Places for the Boxes to be taken of Mr. FOSBROOK, at the
Box-Office, in Little Russell-Street.

N. B. Till further notice, Places can only be taken from
Nine o'Clock, till Three.

NO MONEY TO BE RETURNED.

Vivant Rex et Regina ! [C. Lowndes. Printer at the Theatre

On SATURDAY,
(Being the Last Night of Performing till the Holidays.)
Will be presented the Tragedy of BARBAROSSA,
The Part of *Achmet* by the YOUNG ROSCIUS,
With (21st time) the Romance of RICHARD CŒUR de LION.
☞ The Two First Nights of The YOUNG ROSCIUS's,
Performance in the EASTER WEEK, will be on Tuesday the
16th, and Thursday the 18th of April.

Playbill depicting Betty as *The Young Roscius*

HAMLET.

ACT III. Scene IV.

Ham........Look you now, what follows :
Here is your husband ; like a mildew'd ear,
Blasting his wholesome brother.

Closet Scene of the Kemble Period from Vol 3 of the *Magnet* edition (1834-6)

John Philip Kemble playing Hamlet at Drury Lane after its reconstruction in 1812

Hamlet introduced Mr. Kemble to a London audience, and it may well be doubted whether the part was ever so ably represented either before or since. The calm, contemplative nature of the royal Dane, seemed to sit peculiarly well upon him, and the noble poetry of the part came from his mouth clothed with all the richness and harmony of eloquence. His scene with the Ghost was all that the most critical judgement could require; for without once degenerating into a rant, he was impressive in the highest degree. While the spectre continued before him, his eye was fixed in eager inquiry, and his voice, in the fine abjuration "Angels and ministers of grace defend us!" sinking into a hushed irresolute tone, betrayed the amazement of the speaker. When he heard the tale of his father's murder, a sudden hectic of anger flitted over his pale cheek, but is was succeeded by intense sorrow, as he ejaculated "Alas! poor ghost." The devotedness with which he promised revenge appeared to arise naturally out of the circumstances; but the way in which he sunk on his knees as the phantom vanished, asking by his clasped hands, and imploring looks, the paternal blessing was above praise.

In the play scene his wildly expressed affection towards Ophelia, and his anxious scrutiny of the King, combined with the assumed follies of fatuity, deadened the spectator's perception that the whole was a fiction, and cheated him into a belief that real events were passing before him. In the Closet Scene, his upraidings of Gertrude were finely tempered by the affection he still bore her as a son; but the attitude of dumb dismay in which he stood on the reappearance of the Ghost, would have justified Partridge's criticism in *Tom Jones,* who could find nothing wonderful in Garrick's terror at seeing a spirit. In the last act, when apprised of Ophelia's death, his exclamation 'What, the fair Ophelia?" was given in a tone of such heart-rending pathos that every eye in the audience involuntarily dimmed with tears.

Complete Works of Shakespeare 2 vols. (1838)

Kemble not only was the acknowledged first actor of his time, but he also managed Drury Lane for years and assumed control of Covent Garden after its burning in 1808. Drury Lane was destroyed by fire the next year, and the present great edifice was completed in 1812. Two events of his management are worthy of note. On the day before Napoleon was crowned Emperor, London was in a frenzy over an infant prodigy. On December 1, 1804, Kemble arranged for the appearance at Drury Lane of Master William Henry West Betty, the Young Roscius, who was then thirteen years of age. For weeks the populace fought to see him perform, with receipts for twenty-eight nights amounting to £17,000. The younger Pitt actually adjourned Parliament so the members might witness the young star's portrayal of Hamlet. It was a short-lived madness.

During the autumn season of 1809, Covent Garden was in an uproar. For sixty nights the actors could not be heard. To meet the costly reconstruction bill the Kemble management had advanced the prices. People came to shout, "O.P." (old price), to dance, to sing, to heckle, and to enjoy themselves. Business was good, but the art of the theatre did not flourish. When the prices were lowered Covent Garden returned to normal.

Kemble appeared as Hamlet for the last time on May 17, 1817, when he was sixty. A few weeks later he retired from the stage, the occasion being honored by a public dinner. Despite his three decades of prominence, Kemble's position as an actor had been completely eclipsed by the meteoric rise of Edmund Kean.

V

WITH FLASHES OF LIGHTNING

Edmund Kean
c. 1787-1833

BY A SOMEWHAT FATUOUS CIRCUMLOCUTION one might argue that the revocation of the Edict of Nantes by Louis XIV in 1685 gave David Garrick to England, in that his forebears were Huguenot refugees. More realistically, Edwin Booth was an American because his father, Junius Brutus Booth, came off the loser in his rivalry with Edmund Kean and settled in Maryland.

Kean's career is as dramatic as any to be found in the history of the stage. Rising from hardship and obscurity after many years of discouraging struggle, he was given his first London opportunity during the Drury Lane season of 1814. Just before his appearance as Shylock he exclaimed to his young wife, "If I succeed, I shall go mad!" and, immediately afterward, once their fortune was assured, "and Charles shall go to Eton!" And their son Charles did.

In a few weeks, on March 12, 1814, Kean played Hamlet for the first time in London. He had studied the part since the early years of his enthusiasm for the theatre and knew well how he wished to interpret the Prince. It was characteristic of him, for he cared little about the opinions of the critics. As Hamlet, he was compelled to display his shortness of stature without the protecting cloaks of Shylock or Richard. As an added handicap, Kean's voice, although good in the lower register, was inclined to harshness and cracking in the higher. But the initial disappointment was soon dispelled by agile grace and the brilliance of his acting.

For a discussion of the actor's physical equipment we find the following account in the *Theatrical Inquisitor, and Monthly Mirror* of May, 1815:

> His figure, though small, is neat, and well proportioned; his eyes
> are particularly large, and, when lighted up by efforts of the mind,

A portrait of Edmund Kean painted in 1823

Caricature of Edmund Kean circa 1818

are brilliant beyond conception; their lustre is so deep, so piercing, that it is perfectly visible in the remotest parts of the theatre; every passion that can agitate the heart and brain of man is, at will, reflected in their brightness. His face is long, his forehead high, his upper lip is unusually large and curled, and with him is a most powerful organ of expression; though not altogether unpleasing in a state of quiescence, it still, in some measure detracts from the harmony of his combined features. His nose is rather aquiline, his complexion dark, and the separate features sharp and strongly marked. The most striking of his bodily defects is his hoarse and grating voice; yet it is not altogether inharmonious, and as his enunciation is perfectly distinct, and as it expresses every modification of passion and feeling from the most melting tenderness to the wildest tempest of rage and horror, the defect may easily be pardoned. On some occasions, indeed, it is even an advantage; when it is exalted to its highest key, in the expression of the more tumultuous passages, it has a full, yet broken and piercing tone, that thrills to the very hearts of his audience, and fills the soul with horror.

Among Kean's several new "readings," his returning to kiss the hand of Ophelia after his exit on the line, "To a nunnery, go," was particularly admired. Hazlitt called it "the finest commentary that was ever made on Shakespeare." Kean gave his portrayal of Hamlet eight times out of a first season of seventy nights. He was the new theatrical sensation, the great ones flocked to his dressing room, and the shattered fortunes of Drury Lane were restored.

In his review of Kean's first London Hamlet, Hazlitt wrote in *The Morning Chronicle:*

> High as Mr. Kean stood in our opinion before, we have no hesitation in saying that he stands higher in it (and, we think, will in that of the public), from the powers displayed in this last effort. If it was less perfect as a whole, there were parts in it of a higher cast of excellence than any part of his Richard . . . There is no one line in this play which should be spoken like any one line in Richard, yet Mr. Kean did not appear to us to keep the two characters always distinct. . . . His surprise when he first sees the Ghost, his eagerness and filial confidence in following it, the impressive pathos of his action and voice in addressing it, "I'll call thee Hamlet, *Father,* Royal Dane," were admirable.
>
> Mr. Kean has introduced in this part a *new reading,* as it is called, which we think perfectly correct. In the scene where he breaks from his friends to obey the command of his father, he keeps his sword pointed behind him, to prevent them from following him, instead of holding it before him to protect him from the Ghost. The manner of his taking Guildenstern and Rosencrantz under each arm, under pretence of communicating his secret to them, when he only means

Edmund Kean in the year of his London debut

Wageman, del. — T.Woolnoth, sculp.

MR KEAN, AS HAMLET.

Published 1818, by Simkin & Marshall, Stationers Court, & Chappel, Pall Mall.

Kean in 1818

Kean in 1822

to trifle with them, had the finest effect, and was, we conceive, exactly in the spirit of the character. . . . But whatever nice faults may be found in this scene [with Ophelia], they were amply redeemed by the manner of his coming back after he has gone to the extremity of the stage, from a pang of parting tenderness to press his lips to Ophelia's hand. It had an electrical effect on the house. It was the finest commentary, that was ever made on Shakespeare.

Mrs. Garrick had not been a regular frequenter of the theatre during the Kemble regime, but she was convinced that the rightful successor to her beloved "Davy" had now appeared. She invited Kean to her home, bestowed gifts upon him from her husband's regalia (the jewelry worn by Garrick as Richard III) and even coached him in his playing of Hamlet. Hamlet must deal more roundly with the Queen, she insisted. Kean tried to follow her advice but found no satisfaction in it. He preferred his own Hamlet, and played it throughout his comparatively brief career. Yet some of his other roles, notably Richard III, Shylock, and Sir Giles Overreach, were more admired.

Kean's Hamlet costume was even more colorful than Kemble's. The small painting at the Garrick Club shows puffed sleeves and alternating slashing of red silk and purple velvet, much lace, and a profusion of ribbons and orders. He continued to wear the hat with the waving plume affected by Kemble.

The classic dignity of Kemble as an accepted style of acting fell from favor almost overnight before Kean's devastating brilliance. In some of his scenes the effects of his power were so terrifying that women fainted and had to be carried out of the theatre. Junius Brutus Booth was of this "power" school, but Kean outplayed him. On one occasion he inveigled the elder Booth into playing Othello to his Iago, completely confident that his rival would come out a poor second. The plan worked to perfection.

Yet *The Stage* of 1815 did not entirely capitulate to the power of Kean. The Mr. Young, mentioned at the conclusion, is Charles Mayne Young (1777-1856), another leading actor:

> Hamlet in the hands of Mr. Kean, is a sentimental humorist—he never rises to the dignity of the prince, or the firmness of the philosopher. . . . Mr. Kean does not shine in soliloquy. Give him the actions of the mind, and he can exhibit them—the silent solemn cogitations of the soul may not be beyond his reach; but he has not yet evinced that he possesses the secret of displaying them. In the sarcasm to the king, when he enquires for the dead body of Polonius, and Hamlet replies, "In heaven; send there and look for him, and if your messenger find him not, look for him in the other place yourself," Mr. Kean is too evidently severe. The king must have been insulted by so direct a breach of common decorum. . . . In the scene with Gertrude, Mr. Kean is admirable, his production of the pictures, and his alarm and agitation when the Ghost enters the apartment, are striking specimens of his power. . . . With more, much more experience

THEATRE ROYAL, DRURY-LANE.

This present SATURDAY, March 12, 1814,

Their Majesties Servants will perform (first time this Season) SHAKSPEARE's Tragedy of

HAMLET,

PRINCE OF DENMARK.

Claudius, King of Denmark, Mr. POWELL,
Hamlet, Mr. KEAN,
His first Appearance in that Character.
Polonius, Mr. DOWTON, Laertes, Mr. I. WALLACK,
Horatio, Mr. HOLLAND, Rosencrantz, Mr. CROOKE,
Guildenstern, Mr. FISHER, Osrick, Mr. PALMER,
Marcellus, Mr. MILLER, Bernardo, Mr. RAY,
Francisco, Mr. EVANS, Priest, Mr. CARR,
First Actor, Mr. MADDOCKS, Second Actor, Mr. W. WEST,
First Grave-digger, Mr. BANNISTER,
(His First Appearance in that Character.)
Second Grave-digger, Mr. PENLEY,
First Sailor, Mr. CHATTERLEY, Second Sailor, Mr. I. WEST,
Ghost of Hamlet's Father, Mr. RAYMOND.

Gertrude, Queen of Denmark, Mrs. BRERETON,
Ophelia, Miss SMITH,
(Her First Appearance in that Character.)
Actress, Miss TIDSWELL.

To which will be added a Musical Entertainment called

THE PRIZE;

Or, 2 5. 3. 8.

Lenitive, Mr. BANNISTER,
Mr. Caddy, Mr. MADDOCKS,
Heartwell, Mr. J. SMITH, Label, Mr. OXBERRY,
Juba, Mrs. VINING, (late Miss BEW.)
Servant, Mr. I. WEST, Boy, Master SEYMOUR.
Mrs. Caddy, Miss TIDSWELL,
Caroline, Miss KELLY.

All Persons to whom the Favor has been granted of a Free-Admission to this Theatre, are particularly requested by the Sub-Committee of Management, to abstain from the Use of such Indulgence, on the Nights of Mr. KEAN's Performance.

NO ORDERS WILL BE ADMITTED.
VIVANT REX ET REGINA. NO MONEY TO BE RETURNED. [Lowndes and Hobbs, Marquis Court, London.

The Publick are most respectfully informed, in answer to the continued and unexampled increase of applications for Boxes, Shakspeare's Play of KING RICHARD the THIRD will be repeated on every Monday: and the MERCHANT OF VENICE on every Thursday till further notice.
On Monday, (9th time,) KING RICHARD THE THIRD, King Richard, Mr. KEAN,
With the THREE and the DEUCE.
On Tuesday, the favorite revived Opera of the SIEGE OF BELGRADE, which was received throughout, on Tuesday night, with unbounded applause; the Part of the Seraskier by Mr. BRAHAM. After which the popular Melo-dramatick Romance of ILLUSION, being the last time it can be performed till after the Easter Holidays.
On Wednesday, MOZART's celebrated REQUIEM, Beethoven's New Oratorio of the MOUNT OF OLIVES, and a GRAND MISCELLANEOUS ACT.
On Thursday, (10th time) SHAKSPEARE's Play of the MERCHANT OF VENICE, Shylock, Mr. KEAN.
On Friday, A SACRED ORATORIO.
Early notice will be given of the Production of the New Melo-Dramatick Romance, to be called the WOODMAN'S HUT.

Playbill
Kean's first appearance as Hamlet

49

THEATRE ROYAL, DRURY-LANE.

The last appearance of Mr Kean in Hamlet

Agreeably to the former Advertisement,

THIS THEATRE IS NOW OPEN

For the LAST PERFORMANCES of

Mr. KEAN,

BEFORE HIS *POSITIVE* DEPARTURE FOR

AMERICA.

This Evening, THURSDAY, August 17, 1820,

His Majesty's Servants will perform Shakspeare's Tragedy of

HAMLET.

Claudius, King of Denmark,   Mr. POWELL,
Hamlet,   Mr. KEAN,
(His last appearance in that Character.)
Polonius,   Mr. MUNDEN,
Laertes, Mr. JEFFRIES,   Horatio, Mr. THOMPSON,
Rosencrants, Mr. BROMLEY,   Guildenstern, Mr. VINING,
Ostick,   Mr. RUSSELL,
Marcellus, Mr. RAYMOND,   Bernardo, Mr. MORETON,
Francisco, Mr. HUDSON,   Priest, Mr. READ,
First Actor, Mr. CARR,   Second Actor, Mr. STARMER,
First Grave-digger, Mr. GATTIE,   Second Grave-digger, Mr. HUGHES,
First Sailor, Mr. RANDALL,   Second Sailor, Mr. WILSON,
Ghost of Hamlet's Father, Mr. POPE.
Gertrude, Queen of Denmark,   Mrs. EGERTON,
Ophelia, Miss CUBITT,   Actress, Mrs. PARKER.

VENICE PRESERVED

Was acted before a most brilliant Audience with rapturous Applause:

Mr. KEAN

Was honoured with the usual distinguished demonstrations of the public estimation of his talents;—he will perform JAFFIER *ONCE MORE* before his departure for America. He will appear in HAMLET this Evening *for the last time.*

After which, the Comedy of

Three Weeks after Marriage.

Sir Charles Racket,   Mr. ELLISTON,
Drugget,   Mr. MUNDEN,
Woodley, Mr. VINING,   Servant, Mr. MORETON,
Lady Racket,   Mrs. EDWIN,
Mrs. Drugget, Mrs. HARLOWE,   Nancy, Miss CARR,
Dimity,   Miss CUBITT.

The Doors will be opened at Half-past Six o'Clock, and the Performances on each Evening commence at Seven.

Boxes 7s.   Second Price 3s. 6d.—Pit 3s. 6d.   Second Price 2s.
Lower Gallery 2s.   Second Price 1s.—Upper Gallery 1s.   Second Price 6d.
The Box-Office will be open from 10 till 5 o'Clock; Places to be taken of Mr. RODWELL, Box Book-keeper.

☞ The FREE LIST cannot be extended to these Performances, the PUBLIC PRESS always excepted.

No Money to be returned.   J. Tabby, Printer, Theatre Royal, Drury-Lane.

Mr. KEAN

Will perform *Sir Giles Overreach*, To-morrow Evening; *Othello*, on Saturday; and *King Lear*, on Monday next.

To-morrow, A NEW WAY TO PAY OLD DEBTS.

Sir Giles Overreach,   Mr. KEAN,
Marrall, Mr. MUNDEN,   Wellborn, Mr. RUSSELL.
Lady Allworth, Mrs. EGERTON   Margaret, Mrs. EDWIN.   And the THREE and the DEUCE.
The Three Singles, by Mr. ELLISTON.
On Saturday, OTHELLO, Othello, Mr. KEAN.   Iago, JUNIUS BRUTUS BOOTH,
Cassio, Mr. ELLISTON.   Roderigo, Mr. RUSSELL.
Desdemona, Mrs. W. WEST,   Emilia, Mrs. EGERTON.   With MODERN ANTIQUES.
Cocletop, Mr. MUNDEN, Joey, Mr. RUSSELL, Frank, Mr. W. H. WILLIAMS. Nan, Mrs. EDWIN.
On Monday, KING LEAR.   King Lear, Mr. KEAN,
Edgar, JUNIUS BRUTUS BOOTH,   Cordelia, Mrs. W. WEST.

and reflection, he may yet rescue his failure in some parts [portions], not merely as compared with Mr. Kemble, but with Mr. Young.

A letter to *The Stage* praises Kean's independence:

He consults no stage effects, or disguises his aim so effectually that no one perceives the object. He has no invariable flourish when he enters—no elevation of his hands to the gods of the galleries—no frown at the critical being in the pit. He confines himself to the business of the stage. . . There is no appearance in Kean of even a wish to please. If his efforts succeed, well—if otherwise, he stoops not to adopt any other mode—he will not destroy his own conception of that character, to accommodate the taste of either the many or the few.

A biographer recalls the "almost awful reality" of the death scene:

It had been unusual to show that Hamlet died from the effects of a sword wound, but discriminating with rare intelligence between the manner of death with reference to its cause, Kean conceived that in doing the work of dissolution the rapid agent must have been a powerful mineral, intense internal pain, wandering vision, and distended veins of the temple. His realization of this hypothesis was of an almost awful reality. His eye dilated and then lost its lustre; he gnawed his hand in the vain effort to repress the expression of physical suffering which rose to his countenance; the veins in his forehead swelled and thickened; his limbs shuddered and quivered; his hand dropped from between his stiffening lips, and he uttered a cry of nature so exquisite that it could only be compared to the stifled sob of a fainting woman.

F. W. Hawkins: *The Life of Edmund Kean* (London 1869)

The Examiner complains that the age of chivalry is dead as far as audiences are concerned:

In his representations of Hamlet Mr. Kemble showed an ignorance of character which would have been scarcely pardonable in the first stroller picked up at a country fair. . . In what manner did he treat the fair Ophelia? What threatening of fists, what ferocity of voice, what stamping of feet, what clattering of doors? Had there been one spark of chivalry left among us, the pit and boxes would have sprung on to the stage and dashed to the earth the insolent intruder who could so insult a lovely and harmless woman. But alas! the fashionables in their boxes who hate their wives, and the honest simpletons in the pit who are afraid of theirs, seemed to rejoice in this triumph over the daughter of Polonius as if it had avenged their own particular wrongs. What a striking and amiable contrast was Mr. Kean's management of this encounter. . . He did not shake his mother out of her chair, nor wave his handkerchief with a dignified whirl, nor spread his arms like a heron crucified on a barn-door, when he cries, 'Is it the king?'

In 1820, while still at the height of his fame, Kean made an American tour, the first celebrated English actor to do so. Five years later he made another. He could scarcely be heard above the din of indignant and protesting audiences. They hooted, whistled, and interrupted his lines, while Kean battled through the trying experience, giving back insult for insult with all the rage and scorn of his fiery nature. London had set the example, for scandal and court proceedings resulting in his wife's leaving him had completely alienated the actor in the affections of the public. His tragic degeneration was rapid. The wrath of the populace subsided, but those who attended his later performances saw only diminishing flashes of the power that had once electrified London audiences.

On November 9, 1832, Kean appeared as Hamlet for the last time. There followed sporadic performances in other roles, many of them impaired by illness or canceled by order of his physician. A Covent Garden handbill for March 25, 1833, announced that Kean would play Othello to the Iago of his son Charles, recently reconciled with his father after a long estrangement. Kean had completed the line, "Farewell! Othello's reputation's gone!" when, at the words, "Villain, be sure . . .," he collapsed in the arms of his son. Murmuring, "I'm dying—speak to them for me," the actor was carried from the stage.

It can be properly observed that whereas Kean dominated the first quarter of the nineteenth century, Edwin Forrest and William Charles Macready were secure in the eyes of the theatregoing public during the second.

VI

THE RIOT ACT

Edwin Forrest
c. 1806-1872
—William C. Macready
c. 1793-1873

BY A TRAGIC IRONY, Edwin Forrest and William Charles Macready are inseparably linked in theatre annals. For the bitter rivalry between these leading performers in their respective countries culminated in a fatal riot in New York that cast a pall on their distinguished careers. In the background of the incident lie the animosity and lack of understanding between Americans and Englishmen during the raw days before the Civil War. What Charles Dickens had written about the United States in the 1840's and apologized for in the 1860's was characteristic of this era of ill-feeling.

The earlier acquaintance of Forrest, the American, and Macready, the Englishman, had been of the most friendly nature. Macready entertained the visiting tragedian at the Garrick Club, and it was through him that Forrest met Catharine Sinclair, his future wife. But during his second tour eight years later, both in London and Paris, Forrest was convinced that Macready was hostile to him. The most provocative incident occurred on March 2, 1846, when Macready was playing Hamlet in Edinburgh. Forrest hissed him as he waved the handkerchief just before the Play Scene, a piece of stage business Macready had derived from Garrick ,and thereafter, with his best contempt Forrest referred to it as the *pas de mouchoir*.

Recriminations reached their climax during Macready's third visit to the United States, the feud having produced the most bitter sort of partisanship among audiences. The Englishman was fully aware of the tension and would not have risked the final fatal test of a public appearance but for the intervention of prominent Americans such as Washington Irving.

Edwin Forrest
A painting done in Albany, New York in 1827

Edwin Forrest about 1835

On the night of May 10, 1849, after hours of rioting in and around the Astor Place Opera House, troops were compelled to fire upon the mob. Twenty-two persons were killed and thirty-six wounded. James Henry Hackett, the manager, sustained a loss of $4,400. Macready escaped and immediately returned to England.

For a celebrated actor, Macready maintained a peculiar attitude toward his profession. He was admired and regarded with affection by the great men of his day, yet among the people of the theatre he had few friends. To his hypersensitive nature, the actor was an unworthy fellow and a social outcast. He lived out the last twenty years of his life in a sort of scholarly retirement.

In popular estimation Macready was a good Hamlet. Never thoroughly satisfied with his interpretation of the role, which he first performed at Covent Garden on June 8, 1821, he gave it constant study and attention, and his efforts were well rewarded. Although he possessed some of the dignity of Kemble, his mien and bearing were not altogether princely. In Forrest's eyes:

> He wore a dress the waist of which nearly reached his arms; a hat with a sable plume big enough to cover a hearse; a pair of black silk gloves much too large for him; a ballet shirt of straw-colored satin, which looked simply dirty; and, what with his gaunt, awkward, angular figure, his grizzled hair, his dark beard close-shaven to his square jaws, yet unsoftened by a trace of pigment, his irregular features, his queer extraordinary nose . . . and his long skinny neck, he appeared positively hideous.

After the opening gloom comes this enlightening tribute and final verdict on Macready's voice:

> But, after all, 'mind is the brightness of the body', and, O ye gods! when he spoke, how he brightened, illumined, irradiated the atmosphere.

The Englishman was most effective in the Play and Closet Scenes. By January 9, 1851, his performances of Hamlet in London alone had reached a total of eighty-five.

Of all the great actors who have played Hamlet, Edwin Forrest was the least suited to the role. Even at twenty-three, with a youthful appearance considerably in his favor, he did not entirely succeed. Yet he gave the part the most careful, studious attention and continued to include it in his repertoire. Intellect and voice and acting genius—his Lear was unequaled—were in his favor, but his massive muscularity was a well-nigh insurmountable barrier.

Lessee & Manager - Joseph Leonard | Stage Manager - - J. B. Wright

PRICES OF ADMISSION

DRESS CIRCLE & PARQUETTE - 50 CTS | THIRD CIRCLE - - - - - 25 CTS
SECOND, or FAMILY CIRCLE - 25 CTS | PRIVATE BOXES, SINGLE TICKET, $1.00

Doors open at half-past 6 . . . . Curtain will rise at 7 o'clock.

The Box Office will be open from 10 o'clock every Morning, and Tickets can be procured any time during the day. Tickets may be purchased for any Performance during the week, and seats secured. No Money taken at the door. Checks not transferable.

Benefit

AND POSITIVELY LAST APPEARANCE OF THE

EMINENT AMERICAN TRAGEDIAN
MR

FORREST

Will appear on this occasion in his Great Shaksperian Character of

HAMLET

Pronounced unequalled in excellence since the days of EDMUND KEAN.

ON MONDAY EVENING, February 7, 1853,

Will be performed Shakspere's Sublime Tragedy, entitled

HAMLET!

PRINCE OF DENMARK.

HAMLET . . . . . Mr FORREST

Claudius, King of Denmark,		Priest	Mr Taylor
	Mr W. H. Curtis	Lucianus	Haynes
Laertes	W. M. Leman	Francisco	Lake
Polonius	W F. Johnson	1st Grave Digger	S. D. Johnson
Horatio	Aiken	2d " "	F. S. Buxton
Osric	Wayne Olwine	The Ghost	J. J. Prior
Rosencrantz	F. Aiken	Lords, Officers, Soldiers, &c.	
Guildenstein	G. Johnson	Gertrude, Queen of Denmark. Mrs Vickery	
Marcellus	J. H. Ring	Ophelia	Miss Julia Pelby
Bernardo	Lampee	Ladies	Misses Chisholm, Melvin,
Player King	Munroe	Brown, Sherlock, Watson.	

SYLPHIDE - - - - M'lle C. PALSER

To conclude with the Admired Farce, entitled

SKETCHES IN INDIA!

Sir Matthew Scraggs	Mr W. F. Johnson	Dawkins	Mr Lampee
Capt Dorrington	Aiken		
Dick Milton	F. Aiken	Lady Scraggs	Mrs Archbold
Tom Tape	S. D. Johnson	Sally Scraggs	Mrs W. H. Smith
Count Glorieaux	Lake	Poplin	Mrs F S. Buxton

TUESDAY—1st Night of the New Scottish Drama of the

ROSE OF ETTRICK VALE

Wednesday, Feb. 9—Benefit of Mrs Vickery

IN REHEARSAL, a New Local Farce, written by a Gentleman of Boston, entitled

APPLYING FOR OFFICE.

In Rehearsal, and will shortly be produced, a New Drama in 3 acts, written by a Gentleman of Boston, entitled "THE MAN OF THE PEOPLE."

Morton's Press-Station' Buildings, corner of Howard and Tremont streets.

Playbill
Pronounced unequalled in excellence since the days of Edmund Kean

Forrest in his later years

A great stage career spanning half a century is an achievement. During Edmund Kean's first American tour, Forrest, scarcely more than a school-boy, was making appearances in Philadelphia. An early illustration (not as Hamlet) shows a lad of great personal charm, a rich attribute that, unfortunately, was but fleeting. When Kean came to the United States for the second time, the youthful Forrest met and was briefly associated with him—the apprentice in the presence of the great master. The influence of Kean not only was apparent in Forrest's acting, but in his first Hamlet costume as well. One observes the familiar lace collar and the ribbon and royal insignia around the neck. He later dispensed with these in favor of a more somber knee-length tunic with silk lining of purple or red. A heavy tasseled cord hung from his shoulders to serve as a hanger for the sword.

Forrest's gradual decline in public esteem is attributable to two causes. The first was the sensational nature of his divorce trial; the second, the emergence of a new star in the person of Edwin Booth. Indeed, toward the close of his career Forrest actually played Hamlet in New York against that of young Booth.

The very youthful reviewer John Forster, biographer of Dickens, wrote for *The Examiner* of Oct. 11, 1835:

> Mr. Macready's Hamlet is a noble and beautiful performance. . . Vivid delineations of moments of passion, we have seen equally fine, fragments of possibly superior beauty in the acting of the late Mr. Kean—but never such a grasp of thought, never such a sustained exhibition of single, profound, and enduring passion, cast in the yielding and varying mould of imagination. . . The impassioned and heartbreaking sorrow with which Mr. Macready opened the play in the first soliloquy was a noble foundation for the entire structure of the character.
>
> His manner of turning from Horatio, as he hears the approaching footsteps of the King—"They are coming to the play, I must be idle"—his quick and salient walk up and down the front of the stage, waving his handkerchief as if in idle and gay indifference, but ill-concealing, at that instant, the sense of an approaching triumph—was one of those things Shakespeare himself would have done had he acted Hamlet. The whole scene was masterly. . . As he stands there, in the flushed excitement of a triumph, we feel that he is satisfied with the discovery alone.
>
> We conclude as we began by characterising Mr. Macready's performance of Hamlet as the most perfect achievement of the modern stage—in depth, in originality, in truth, in beauty, and in grandeur of sustainment.

Forrest in the Play Scene

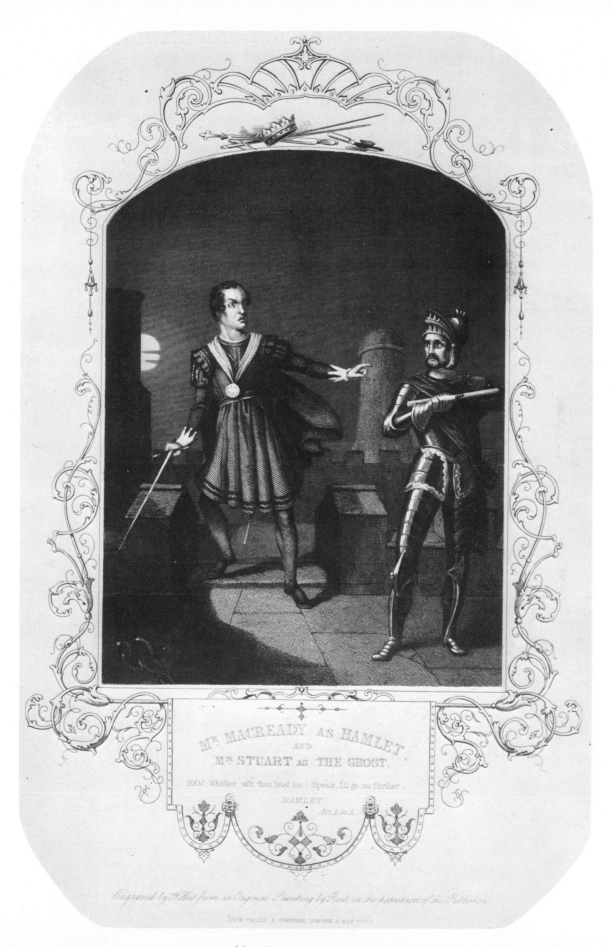

Mr MACREADY AS HAMLET
AND
Mr STUART AS THE GHOST.

HAM: Whither wilt thou lead me ! Speak, I'll go no further.

HAMLET.
Act 1 Sc 5.

Engraved by Hollis from an Original Painting by Reid in the possession of the Publishers.

JOHN TALLIS & COMPANY LONDON & NEW YORK

Macready in the Ghost Scene

Macready as Hamlet at the Princess Theatre, London

Henry F. Chorley, a sensitive critic, who for some time was in charge of the music department of *The Times,* made an interesting distinction on the occasion of Forrest's first London engagement:

> However much Macready nerves one at the time by the subtle intellect of his personifications, I am never much better for it afterwards—never find a word, a look, or an attitude written on my heart. There are certain points of Mr. Forrest's playing that I shall never forget, to my dying day.

Neither Forrest nor Macready was born to play Hamlet. We quote Lawrence Barret on the former:

> Hamlet, Richard, and Macbeth were out of his temperament, and added nothing to his fame.
>
> Edwin Forrest (1881)

and George Henry Lewes, eminent litterateur and husband of George Eliot, on the latter:

> Although you can see him in no part without feeling that an artist is before you, yet if you think of him as a great actor, it is as Werner, Lear, Virginus, Richelieu, King John, Richard II, Iago—not as Othello, Macbeth, Hamlet, Coriolanus.
>
> The Leader (February 8, 1851)

* * * *

> His Hamlet I thought bad, due allowance being made for the intelligence it displayed. He was lachrymose and fretful: too fond of a cambric pocket-handkerchief to be really affecting.
>
> On Actors and the Art of Acting (London 1875)

The American comedian James Henry Hackett, notable for his Falstaff, has written descriptions of Macready and Forrest that convey infinitely more than drawings or photographs:

> Mr. Macready in *propria persona,* minutely surveyed, is above the middle height, his port rather stiffly erect, his figure, not stout but very straight, and at the hips quite the reverse of *en bon point,* his ordinary or natural gait is not dignified; his steps short and quick with a springy action of the knee joints, which sometimes trundling his stiff bust—as in a rush from the centre to a corner of the stage— reminds one of the recoil of a cannon upon its carriage; in his slow and measured tread of the stage, he seems somewhat affected: he sags his body alternately on either leg, whilst his head waves from side to side to balance it: his head, however, is not unproportioned, and his hair is of a dark brown; his face, though occasionally lighted up by a pleasing smile, can hardly have beauty predicated of it: his forehead is good, but his brow . . . rather high, vacant, and irregularly arched though not inflexible; his eyes are blue, of good size, widely set and tolerably effective in his acting; though he has a trick of turning them upward rather too frequently and dropping his chin upon

Macready in the Play Scene
From the painting by Maclise

Macready at the Tuilleries in Paris in 1845

Macready in the Gravediggers Scene

his breast; half covering the eye-balls with the upper lids and leaving the whites below well-defined, looks too much aghast when he would express reverential awe; his nose is of ordinary length, rather low and straight from his forehead down to beneath its bridge, where it abruptly rises; his mouth is not remarkable and his chin is prominent, his voice is tolerably strong, but without volume or much compass; when sunk it is sometimes monotonous, and when raised often becomes quite reedy . . . his legs are rather long and thin by *nature,* but being straight are proportioned at stage by his art, and his arms are more bony than brawny; his actions are generally formal and sometimes more angular than graceful; but, with all Mr. Macready's personal disadvantages, his discerning mind and untiring industry have so disciplined his physique, that, "take him for all in all," I consider him by far the most intellectual and generally effective actor of the time.

*   *   *   *

Mr. Forrest's own *propria facies* is what may be classed in its *ensemble* "handsome", though the nose is a little too small, crooked, and short, to be symmetrical. Nature has given him pleasing black eyes, too, which, however, he seems not to have acquired the art to make specially effective on the stage—possibly because his inflexible brows, which arch low and near the bridge of the nose, impart when pursed together a grim severity to his countenance . . . his person generally, with his ample chest, long body, short and Herculean-proportioned arms and legs, does not conform to the ideal of an Apollo; nor is his ease, or grace of action, or carriage of body, remarkable or conventionally well-adapted to represent "the glass of fashion and the mould of form." Mr. Forrest's voice is strong, but appears not susceptible of much modulation, though his articulation is good, and his general physique denotes extraordinary animal strength.

Notes and Comments upon Certain Plays and Actors of Shakespeare
(New York 1863)

Forrest's biographer, W. R. Alger, gave way before the spell of his subject's Hamlet:

The clear good sense, the trained professional skill, and the deep personal experience of Forrest gave him an accurate perception of the general character of Hamlet. . . And in rendering it he did all he could to neutralize the ill-adaptedness of his stalwart person and abounding vigor for the philosophical and romantic sentimentality of the part by a subdued and pensive manner and a costume which made his figure appear more tall and slender. He laid aside the massive hauteur of his port, and walked the stage and conversed with his interlocutors as a thoughtful scholar would walk the floor of his library and talk with his friends. Even when he broke into passionate indignation or scorn a restraining power of culture and refinement curbed the violence.

Forrest endeavored to represent in their truth the rapid succession of transitory and contradictory moods of Hamlet and yet never lose the central thread of unity on which they were strung.

Of all who have acted the part no one perhaps has ever done such complete justice to the genius of Hamlet as Forrest did in his noble delivery of the great speeches and soliloquies, with full observance of every requirement of measure, accent, inflection, and relative importance of thought . . . the voice of Forrest brought the very objects spoken of before the hearer,—the good frame, the earth; the most excellent canopy, the air . . . he altered the tone of admiration to a tone of awe, his speech stirred the soul like the grandest chords in the Requiem of Mozart, thrilling it with sublime premonitions of its own infinity.

Life of Edwin Forrest (Lippincott, Philadelphia, 1877)

Forrest and Macready fade into the past, and a star of the first magnitude is about to capture the attention of theatregoers.

VII

TAKE HIM FOR ALL IN ALL

Edwin Booth
1833-1893

THERE IS NO NAME in the history of the American theatre more indelibly associated with Hamlet than that of Edwin Booth. He made his first appearance as the Prince in San Francisco in 1852, and his last at the Brooklyn Academy of Music in 1891. During this period of nearly four decades, throughout the United States, in Europe, and even in Australia, audiences saw and admired Booth's Hamlet.

His phenomenal success is not difficult to account for. He looked the part; he was gifted in voice, and he had inherited from his father, Junius Brutus Booth, a sense of the stage. But most of all he was by nature of the very substance of Hamlet—kindly, courteous, gentlemanly, possessed with a natural dignity—and he knew sorrow.

In the autumn of 1864, Booth opened his season with *Hamlet,* at the old Winter Garden in New York. A record run of one hundred nights resulted.

For comment on the young Hamlet period we cite three passages. The first is by "Nym Crinkle" (Andrew C. Wheeler) of *The New York World* from *The Primrose Path of Dalliance; a Story of the Stage* (1892):

> The real truth about Mr. Edwin Booth's Hamlet, at this time, is that he was immature in thought and unoriginal in conception. It reflected, in a confused way, the traditions both of Kemble and of the actor's father. But it was absolutely free from all the blemishes of Forrest. It wavered in its eclecticism from one conception to another, as if the young man had no positive conviction of his own concerning the interpretation of the text, but it was unique in its declamatory discretion, and as sharp as an antique cameo in its presentment of a nimble, nervous and melancholy youth. In the matter

As Hamlet from an original painting by John Pope.

Edwin Booth
From a painting by John Pope

Booth in his distinctive Hamlet Costume (1870's)

Edwin Booth in two photographs of his earlier period

of intrinsic intellectuality, Mr. Forrest's Hamlet was, in my opinion, superior to Mr. Booth's. In the illusion of intellectuality, Mr. Booth's was altogether the most acceptable and, so far as the public at the time was concerned, if it was not a revelation, it was nevertheless a relief.

George William Curtis wrote of his one hundred nights at the Winter Garden:

> Booth is altogether princely. His costume is still the solemn suit of sables, varied according to his fancy of greater fitness; and his small lithe form, with mobility and intellectual sadness of his face, and his large melancholy eyes, satisfy the most fastidious imagination that this is Hamlet as he lived in Shakespeare's world.
>
> With sword uplifted, and a vague terror both of hope and fear in his tone and face, Hamlet does not slide rapidly back, and hurriedly exclaim, 'Is it the king?' but, tottering with emotion, he asks slowly in an appalling staccato, 'Is - it - the - king?' The cumulative sadness of the play was never so palpable as in Booth's acting. It is a spell from which you cannot escape.

Two years later there appeared this little item in *The Boston Traveller* of Sept. 18, 1866:

> Mr. Booth has three things in his favor: youth, the name he bears, and beauty; he is a favorite with the ladies, and their verdict is omnipotent. After seeing his performance they look upon Hamlet as perfection, whereas he was about as contemptible a whelp as ever breathed.

While Booth was repeating his New York success in Boston, the news that his brother John Wilkes had assassinated President Abraham Lincoln was handed to him. This shock, coming only two years after the death of his wife, to whom he was completely devoted, prompted Booth to announce his retirement. But the insistent urging of friends and public alike brought him back to the stage the following January and wild excitement and a tumultuous ovation. In the immediate years that lay ahead Booth was to suffer the loss of his theatre by fire and of his fortune in the financial panic of 1873.

Lest our praise of Booth be thought fulsome, let us quote from *The Boston Traveler* of December 1, 1869: "Hamlet is a part which he cannot nor never could act." It is true that Booth's performances were often uneven. He could not, on every occasion, exercise his soul to the point of incandescence. William Winter has written that no one could know Booth's acting who had not seen him play the same part several times. It is also true that he attained an ever finer mastery of Hamlet, gave up many of the artificialities of earlier days, and understood more thoroughly

BOSTON THEATRE.

THOMAS BARRY · · · LESSEE AND MANAGER | J. B. WRIGHT · · · · ASSISTANT MANAGER

EDWIN BOOTH

The Manager has the pleasure of announcing an Engagement for a limited number of Nights
with the above

YOUNG AMERICAN TRAGEDIAN!

"*Fresh from his Southern Triumphs.*"

Who will make his Second Appearance in his Celebrated Character of

HAMLET

MRS. HUDSON KIRBY as	· · · · · · ·	**OPHELIA**
MRS. ABBOTT as	· · · · · · ·	**THE QUEEN**
MR. JOHN GILBERT as	· · · · · · ·	**POLONIUS**
MR. W. DAVIDGE as	· · · ·	**THE GRAVE-DIGGER**
MR. J. B. HOWE as	· · · · · · ·	**LAERTES**
MR. W. A. DONALDSON as	· · · · ·	**THE KING**
MR. DAVENPORT as	· · · · · · ·	**HORATIO**

Mr. W. Davidge, Mr. W. H. Curtis, Mr. Davenport,
Miss Ida Vernon and Mrs. John Gilbert,
IN THE FARCE!

☞ NOTICE.—A Box in the Second Tier has been assigned for the use of Colored Persons, who
can only be admitted to that part of the Theatre.

Private Boxes, · · · · · · $6.00 ‖ Family Circle, · · · · · · 25 cts.
Parquette, Balcony, and First Tier of Boxes, 50 cts. ‖ Amphitheatre, · · · · · · 15 cts.

Doors Open at 1-2 past 6 o'clock.   Performance will Commence at 7.

This, Wednesday Evening, · · · · March 24, 1858,

Will be performed Shakespeare's Sublime Tragedy of

HAMLET!

HAMLET, by · · · · · · · · · · · Mr. EDWIN BOOTH
Second Night of his Engagement.

THE GHOST, by	Mr. BARRY
THE KING, by	Mr. W. A. DONALDSON
POLONIUS, by	Mr. JOHN GILBERT
LAERTES, by	Mr. J. B. HOWE
OSRIC, by	Mr. S. D. JOHNSON
HORATIO, by	Mr. DAVENPORT
ROSENCRANTZ, by	Mr. G. JOHNSON
GUILDENSTERN, by	Mr. SELWIN
MARCELLUS, by	Mr. PRICE
PLAYER KING, by	Mr. COWELL
FIRST GRAVE DIGGER, by	Mr. W. DAVIDGE
SECOND GRAVE DIGGER, by	Mr. FINN
PRIEST, by	Mr. VERNEY
BERNARDO, by	Mr. ROSE
FRANCISCO, by	Mr. DAYMOND
LUCIANUS, by	Mr. HOLMES

Lords, Actors, Guards, &c.

GERTRUDE, The Queen, by	Mrs. ABBOTT
PLAYER QUEEN, by	Miss IDA VERNON
Ophelia, by	**Mrs. Hudson Kirby**

To Conclude with a new Comic Drama, by the Celebrated Farce Writer, J. Maddison Morton, called the

TWO BUZZARDS!

JOHN SMALL, by	Mr. W. DAVIDGE
GLIMMER, by	Mr. DAVENPORT
BENJAMIN BUZZARD	Mr. W. H. CURTIS
LUCRETIA BUZZARD	Mrs. J. GILBERT
SALLY, by	Miss IDA VERNON

THURSDAY—Third Night of the Young American Tragedian

EDWIN BOOTH,

And First Night of

WISEMAN MARSHALL,

Fourth Night of

MRS. HUDSON KIRBY,

Who will appear in Shakespeare's Tragedy of **OTHELLO!**

IAGO, by · · · · · · · · · Mr. EDWIN BOOTH
The only Night in which he will appear in that Character during his present brief Engagement.

OTHELLO, by · · · · · · Mr. WISEMAN MARSHALL
is 1st ap . . . his Season.

CASSIO, by	Mr. J. B. HOWE
BRABANTIO, by	Mr. W. A. DONALDSON
RODERIGO, by	Mr. W. DAVIDGE
EMILIA, by	Mrs. ABBOTT
Desdemona, by	**Mrs Hudson Kirby**

With other Entertainments.

FRIDAY—BENEFIT of EDWIN BOOTH, on which occasion he will appear as *RICHARD III*
SATURDAY AFTERNOON—EDWIN BOOTH.

Playbill
Booth "fresh from his Southern triumphs"

74

Booth in the Play Scene about 1864

its exacting demands. His many years on the road brought endless audiences under the spell of his melancholy Prince. He played it in every sort of theatre imaginable, from the drafty stages of pioneer towns to Henry Irving's Lyceum, with strutting, fretting players, and all-star casts.

The staging for *Hamlet* that Booth ordered to be designed for his theatre was the most elaborate and impressive of its time and served as a model for many succeeding productions. Interiors were massively architectural and imposing. Even the Booth chair became a sort of Hamlet symbol for the actors who followed him. Booth's costume remained a strong influence in dressing the part. He substituted a heavy chain at the neck for the familiar ribbons of Kemble and Kean and others, and adopted cross-gartering.

Fortune did not smile on Booth's tours in England. The first was in 1861, not a propitious time for the London debut of an American actor, coming on the heels of the Hamlet of Charles Fechter, which had already aroused great enthusiasm. Booth fared better in 1880, when the British public had its Hamlet in Henry Irving. The relations between Booth and Irving were completely antithetical to those of Forrest and Macready; their performances, alternating in the roles of Othello and Iago, with Ellen Terry as Desdemona, were among the finest that the stage has known.

A criticism of Booth's second London visit:

> He is said by some to be the mere traditional follower of the "old school" of acting. . . By others we are told that he is "stagey". . . Again, by others, we are told that he is "tricky.".
>
> Instead of being the slave of tradition I found him constantly neglecting old traditional points—of which his manner after the "Play Scene", when his exultation would not give him time to wait until the crowd had wholly dispersed, was, perhaps, the most notable example—for effects which commended themselves better to his true matured intelligence. . . Throughout he was the Prince, without any display of stilted dignity, but graceful in his courtesy and gentlemanly in his condescension. . . His exquisite tenderness towards Ophelia, to whom the words, "Go to a nunnery," were uttered as the warning advice of a man who really loved her, and not as indignant denunciation, was such as to reach every heart.
>
> Another instance may be given on his delivery of the words, "I'll rant as well as thou," which were not howled and ranted, as is commonly the case, but uttered with a profound contempt for the ranting of Laertes. To my mind, Edwin Booth was eminently natural and to be looked upon as an admirable exponent of the more approved new school.
>
> J. Palgrave Simpson *The Theatre* (December 1, 1880)

The Queen's Closet for Edwin Booth's production.
Scene design by Charles Witham

Booth in Scene with Ophelia

By 1882 Booth was accepted as one of the leaders of his profession. In Germany, where without knowledge of the language he acted with German companies who spoke their native tongue, it was not a case of acceptance, but of national acclamation.

Similarly the great Italian actor, Tommaso Salvini, made several American tours, joining Booth's company on occasion to play his greatest role, Othello, to the Iago of Booth. Further distinction and success came to Edwin Booth toward the close of his career in his association with Lawrence Barrett, a high mark in both acting and managerial ability.

William Winter, inveterate writer on the theatre, and Harvard University's Professor Charles Townsend Copeland give their estimates in retrospect.

> Booth's impersonation of Hamlet was one of the best known works of the dramatic age.
>
> In each of Booth's performances a distinguishing attribute was simplicity of treatment, and that was significantly prominent in his portrayal of Hamlet. The rejection of all singularity and the avoidance of all meretricious ornament resulted in a sturdy artistic honesty, which could not be too much admired. The figure stood forth, distinct and stately, in a clear light. The attitudes, gestures, and facial play combined in a fabric of symmetry and of always adequate expression.
>
> To Hamlet the dreamer, Booth usually gave more emphasis than to Hamlet the sufferer—wisely remembering therein the value of stage effect for an audience. . . He moved with grace; he spoke the text with ease, polish, spontaneous fluency, and rich and strong significance . . . But he crowned all by denoting, with incisive distinctness and with woeful beauty, the pathetic vitality of the Hamlet experience.
>
> Booth was an actor of uncertain impulses and conditions, and he was rightly understood only by those who saw him often, in any specified character. Like all persons of acute sensibility, he had his good moments and his bad ones—moments when the genial fire of the soul was liberated, and moments when the artistic faculties could only operate in the hard, cold mechanism of professional routine. Sometimes he seemed lethargic and indifferent. At other times he would put forth uncommon power, and in the ghost scenes and the great third act, would create a thrilling illusion and lift his audience into noble excitement.
>
> Hamlet fascinates by his personality; and no man can succeed in presenting him who does not possess in himself that peculiar quality of fascination. It is something that cannot be drawn from the library, or poured from the flagon, or bought in the shops. Booth possessed it—and that was the first cause of his great success in the character. . .
> If I were to pause upon special points in the execution — I should

Sketch by Thomas Glessing of the Ghost Scene at the Booth Theatre in 1870

Booth during final London engagement

indicate the subtlety with which, almost from the first, the sense of being haunted was conveyed to the imagination; the perfection with which the weird and awful atmosphere of the ghost-scenes was preserved, by the actor's transfiguration into tremulous suspense and horror; the human tenderness and heartbreaking pathos of the scene with Ophelia; the shrill, terrific cry and fate-like swiftness and fury that electrified the moment of killing Polonius; and the desolate calm of despairing surrender to bleak and cruel fate, with which Hamlet, as he stood beside the grave of Ophelia, was made so pitiable an object that no man with a heart in his bosom could see him without tears. Those were peaks of majesty in Booth's interpretation.

William Winter (1893): *Life and Art of Edwin Booth*

* * * *

As to Booth's Hamlet. In the first place his father was right: he "looked like Hamlet." . . . at almost any juncture of the play, indeed, Booth's picture would have made a portrait of the Prince of Denmark.

Booth's performance of the character, as a whole, probably kept to the last more of his early artificiality than was allowed to linger in other roles; more of the mannerisms, or shall one say manner, of the old school. Moved by a laudable wish to preserve the imaginative remoteness of Hamlet, Booth began (and long continued) to play the part on stilts. Trustworthy observers noted, however, that, as time went on, he grew less and less stilted. A great comedian once said in my hearing that he preferred Booth's later Hamlet because "he left out so much" - in other words because he simplified the poses, actions, gestures, and "business" of the performance. . . The gradual change was strikingly exemplified in the tenderness of Hamlet's manner toward Horatio, after the first act; in the seemingly spontaneous grace of his speech to the players; and in the enlivening without hurt to dignity, of his last colloquy with Rosencrantz and Guildenstern. Toward all his inferiors this Hamlet grew more gentle, and in his whimsical talk with the Gravedigger the gentleness was tinged with a sense of humor, that yet never lost the sense of rank. After years of the usual sardonic tone toward Polonius, Booth's Hamlet came to recognize that, though the Lord Chamberlain is a tedious old man, he is also Ophelia's father.

More often than any other of his performances within my recollection, he smote his brow, tragedian fashion, to signify deep thought. . . and, though long before I saw Booth, he had exempted himself from the reproach of "making statues all over the stage," he was, perhaps, as Hamlet, too fond of attitudes that — perfect in their grace — had a pictorial rather than a dramatic significance.

But, whatever many persons deemed the faults of Booth's method, whatever some persons deemed the defects of his conception, the countervailing excellences of the impersonation, regarded as a whole, distinguished Booth's Hamlet as the best that was known to the generation familiar with it. He thoroughly, almost constitutionally, it may be said, felt the deep essentials of the character; and he played it in a manner inexpressibly noble.

When he spoke the words
And for my soul, what can it do to that,
Being a thing immortal as itself?
his face lighted, his voice rang with the certainty of an authentic revelation. Yet over the whole characterization hung, like a dark vapor, the sense of tragic fate.

Charles Townsend Copeland: *Edwin Booth*
(Small, Maynard & Co. Boston 1901)

The Englishman J. Ranken Towse, who was for more than fifty years dramatic critic of *The New York Evening Post,* wrote of Booth's Hamlet for *The Saturday Review of Literature.* His comments of comparison with other interpretations are of special interest:

As a whole it was a notably fine embodiment, remarkable for its general consistency and artistic polish — the best of its generation. Personally, save for its unfortunate foreign intonation, the writer preferred the impersonation of Charles Fechter, not because of its blond wig—which was doubtless correct, in spite of the ridiculous fuss made over it—but because of its general form and character, its more romantic coloring, and its glow of human passion. And it had a flavor of originality. Booth's Hamlet followed traditional lines more closely, as did that of Forbes-Robertson, of which the most striking attributes were dignity and eloquence. He was the last of the "old school" players, being linked with Samuel Phelps, of Sadler's Wells fame. Since his day the only Hamlet of note has been that of Walter Hampden, the most human of them all.

October 22, 1932.

The memory of Edwin Booth as Hamlet, and in his many notable roles, but above all as a man, is revered by The Players, the club he founded. The Macready disregard of his fellow players was completely foreign to Booth. In his opinion the call to the stage was as valid as that to the law or church or medicine, to the making of books or the development of the creative faculties in works of art.

Long desirous of serving the members of his profession in some special way, he achieved this ambition in 1888, five years before his death, in the form of a house for The Players. A residence was acquired, on the south side of Gramercy Park in New York, and there for more than three generations actors have been in friendly association with men of the other arts and professions. Booth became its gracious host, and left within its walls a rich measure of his spirit.

VIII

THE HAMLET OF THE BLOND WIG

Charles Albert Fechter
1824-1879

AN ACTOR WHO in several metropolitan centers seriously challenged Booth's Hamlet was Charles Fechter, yet his name does not loom large today.

Born of an Italian mother and a German father, and reared in France, Fechter became the leading Paris actor of his day. After more than a decade as the reigning favorite, Fechter crossed the Channel in 1860 and amazed and delighted the London audiences by playing superbly in English. There were opening performances in other roles, and finally Hamlet, which on May 20, 1861, immediately established itself for a run of 115 nights at the Princess's Theatre. Nothing like this had been known before. Samuel Phelps, who had rivaled Macready and Charles Kean in Shakespearean interpretations, soon gave ground before the new sensation.

Two contemporary English critics, George Henry Lewes and Dutton Cook, consider Fechter's Hamlet pre-eminent, and dwell upon certain details of interpretation:

> His Hamlet was one of the very best, and his Othello one of the very worst I have ever seen. On leaving the theatre after "Hamlet," I felt once more what a great play it was, with all its faults, and they are gross and numerous.
>
> If Shakespeare's grandest language seemed to issue naturally from Fechter's lips, and did not strike you as out of place, which it so often does when mouthed on the stage, the reason was that he formed a tolerably true conception of Hamlet's nature, and could *represent* that conception. . . Fechter is lymphatic, delicate, handsome, and with his long, flaxen curls, quivering, sensitive nostrils, fine eye, and sympathetic voice, perfectly represents the graceful prince. . . Seldom have the scenes with the players, with Polonius, with Horatio, with Rosencrantz or Guildenstern, or the quieter monologues, been better played;

Charles Fechter during appearance in United States

they are touched with so cunning a grace, and manner so *natural,* that the effect is delightful. . . Yet so great is the power of true emotion that even *this* [the difficulties of a French accent] is forgotten directly he touches the feelings of the audience, and in his great speech,

"O! what a rogue and peasant slave am I!" no one hears the foreigner. . . . It is only in the more tragic scenes that we feel any shortcoming.

George Henry Lewes (London 1875): *On Actors and The Art of Acting*

* * * *

Fechter's Hamlet will long be reckoned by playgoers among the best Hamlets they have ever known.

Dutton Cook (London 1883): *Hours With the Players*

In the play-scene Fechter's Hamlet, when he rose at the discomfiture of Claudius, tore the leaves from the play-book and flung them in the air; in the scene with Ophelia, Fechter's Hamlet did not perceive that the King was watching him; had he known *that* he would have been so convinced of his uncle's guilt that the play would have been unnecessary. In the fourth act, if Fechter's Hamlet had not been well guarded he would have killed the King then and there. In the last scene a gallery ran at the back of the stage with short flights of stairs on either side; all exits and entrances were made by means of these stairs. Upon the confession of Laertes, the King endeavored to escape up the right-hand staircase; Hamlet perceiving this, rushed up the left-hand stairs, and encountering Claudius in the centre of the gallery, there dispatched him.

Dutton Cook (October 1, 1879): *The Theatre*

Fechter's innovations in staging and costuming are recorded in *The Times* of London, of May 23, 1864:

Mr. Fechter has presented his audience with massive architecture of the Norman style, and the dresses of the medieval period. Rosencrantz and Guildenstern are no longer attired in that conventional costume which is vaguely associated with the courtiers of Spain and Italy, but are dressed like Northern warriors — bluff fellows, with thick beards, coarse leggings, and cross garters, and the other personages are after the same model, Mr. Fechter of course retaining that peculiar black dress and blond hair which became so famous at the Princess's.

Over the signature of Herman Merivale in *The Theatre* for Nov. 1, 1897, appears this statement:

In what a wonderful fashion of his own, the Frenchman, Fechter, swept us off our feet, in defiance of law and order at the time laid down. He was the very prince of romantic actors, and treated the play like a romance.

Charles Dickens, who could make his ghosts seem as real as Shakespeare's, penned a sentence of interest to us:

Mr. Fechter's Hamlet—a pale, woe-begone Norseman, with long flaxen hair, wearing a strange garb never associated with the part upon the English stage (if ever seen there at all), and making a piratical swoop upon the whole fleet of little theatrical prescriptions without meaning, or, like Dr. Johnson's celebrated friend, with only one idea in them, and that a wrong one—never could have achieved its extraordinary success but for its animation by one pervading purpose to which all changes were made intelliegntly subservient.

A decade after his London success, Fechter was off for the United States. Here his reception was equally enthusiastic, particularly in Boston. Comparison with Booth inevitably arose, with many considering Fechter's Hamlet superior. In temperament the comparison was far less favorable; Fechter was always extremely difficult in his theatrical associations. Somehow his reputation has paled with the passage of time, while Booth's has brightened. Few Americans can now identify the name of Charles Fechter. In one way certainly the explanation is obvious. His seasons in America, limited to the large cities of the eastern seaboard, can be counted on the fingers of one hand.

It is the more remarkable that Fechter made his impression on audiences in the East when nearing the age of fifty. He was not building on a memory of what he had been as a young Prince, but rather making appearances when, on the face of it, he was much too old for the part. His production of *Hamlet,* in its attempt to simulate more literally the barbarian times, was original to a degree. It must surely have been of some influence on the still youthful Booth when British audiences refused to be aroused over his own version of the play.

Fechter returned to London briefly in 1872, long enough to observe a distinct waning in popularity. He was no longer a young Hamlet, if indeed he ever could have been so considered. Two years later, having deserted his French wife, Fechter married a member of his American company and settled in the United States. Like Edmund Kean, he suffered a decline in health and stage presense in his final seasons. Embittered and neglected by his public, he died on his farm at Quakertvania, Pennsylvania.

To the minds of Hamlet reviewers Fechter remains as the actor who played the part in a flowing, flaxen-haired wig and a tuft of beard. But he was much more than a superficial impersonator. His conception of the role was based on the most minute study, a partial result of which was to make Hamlet a Dane and those who appeared with him members of the Danish Court of an era long before Shakespeare's time. Mere dress does not create the reputation of a great actor, and basing an appraisal upon the somewhat sentimental and stilted studio portraits of the past can give rise to further faulty judgment. We must accept the verdict of those who saw him. Fechter was graceful, a consummate fencer; he offended very few with his slight trace of accent, and was charmingly natural in his dialogue. His soliloquies, particularly the quieter ones, were beyond praise.

Kate Field, journalist and eccentric actress, published Fechter's biography in Boston in 1882:

> Fechter's Hamlet was not the introspective student of tradition. He was a man of the world, in the noblest sense of the term, of joyous disposition, whose temper—and here he agreed with Goethe —assumed its mournful tinge upon the death of his father and the unseemly marriage of his mother.
>
> In the art of fencing Fechter was consummate; consequently the final scene was full of spirit and interest. . . There was no contortion in Fechter's manner of dying. Edmund Kean was no doubt right in illustrating a death by poison; but if Hamlet dies thus, surely Laertes must meet his doom in like manner. Two such exhibitions would be beyond human endurance; and, as Laertes dies first, Hamlet's effects would be lost. Therefore Fechter was not without reason in abstaining from literalness.
>
> Fechter was thoroughly manly . . . Fechter was robust without being unpleasantly so; he was graceful, supple as an athlete, courtly, wondrously picturesque; as his beautiful flaxen wig so transformed his coloring as to cause his dark-hazel eyes to be mistaken for blue.
>
> Possessing good height, small hands and feet, a face so like Garrick's in contour and complexion as in a Garrick wig to render the resemblance astonishing. . . with a large magnetic everchanging hazel eye, with a rich melodious voice that ran the gamut of the passions, with abundant sentiment and humor equally developed, with a sculptor's knowledge of form, a painter's love of costume and color, and a Frenchman's education in the best school of acting, Fechter took his place among the few great actors of the world.
>
> *C. A. Fechter* (Boston 1882)

The links in the Hamlet tradition become closely forged. Booth continued his portrayal long after Fechter, and already the name Irving was to be reckoned with.

IX

FIRST KNIGHT OF THE THEATRE

Sir Henry Irving
1838-1905

IN A CURTAIN SPEECH on December 30, 1878, Henry Irving said: "What you have seen tonight has been the ambition of my life." He had succeeded in producing a *Hamlet* that was to draw audiences for 200 performances. Ellen Terry was his Ophelia. For Irving and Terry there followed a golden era of notable productions at the Lyceum Theatre. Touring the provinces and making several visits to the United States, they attained equally high levels of distinction.

Irving did not risk his Hamlet before a London audience until he had struggled for nearly two decades in the school of the theatre. He first played the part at the age of twenty-six in Manchester. After ten more years of apprenticeship, he took the crucial test, opening at the Lyceum on October 31, 1874. Critical opinion was at opposite poles. "Well might the people shout, for an ideal Hamlet has been found at last," said one. "Mr. Irving is, of all distinguished actors, the least inspired," wrote another. Behind a cloak of anonymity, William Archer, still in his student days, attacked Irving bitterly, even scurrilously. Archer's pen was venomous, and that of his caricaturist even more so. They left poor Irving with scarce an awkward leg to stand on. Bernard Shaw was another dissenter. In spite of the critics, however, theatregoers liked Irving's Hamlet immensely, and it became one of his most favored roles.

Clement Scott exulted in the new Hamlet:

> Henry Irving does not make his success by 'points,' but by a consistent, thoughtful, and highly intelligent reading of the whole character. It is not to be an actor's, but a student's success. . . Well might the people shout, for an ideal Hamlet has been found at last. The

Henry Irving
From the painting by Edwin Long, R.A.

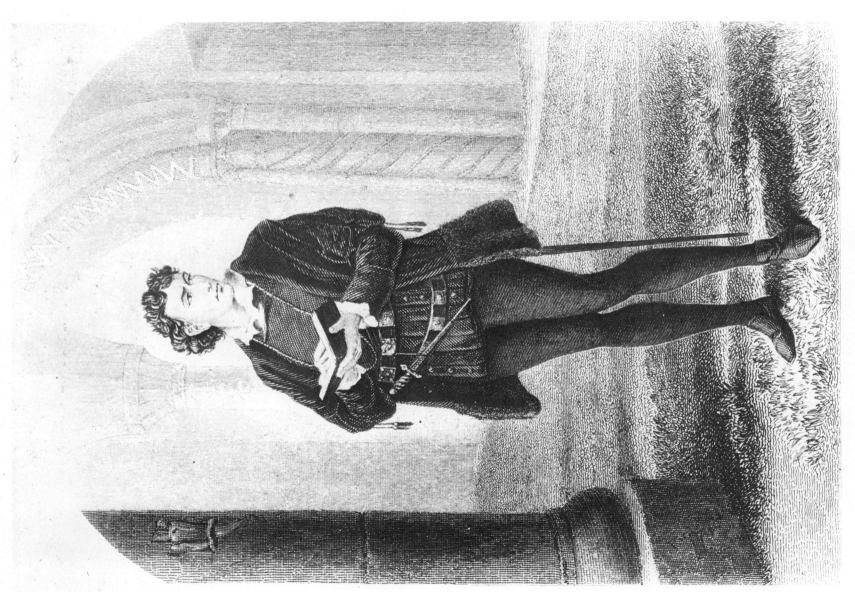

Irving at his first London appearance

scene with the recorders, which proved a daring exhibition of cynicism and contempt; the reaction after the hideous mental depression; and the closet scene, where Mr. Irving defied tradition, and astonished his audience by describing *imaginary* pictures ('Look here upon this picture, and on this'), concluded an act as terrible in its work as it was triumphant on the part of the artist.

And after Irving's second American tour Scott wrote:

He never played Hamlet better, never nearly so well. The old rule was reversed. America sent us back a better actor than the one who left our shores. . . In this revival Mr. Irving had enlarged, rounded off, and polished his original conception of Hamlet. He added to it the rich result of a matured intelligence and a ripened understanding. . . He brought out far more clearly than before his view of the intensely affectionate nature of Hamlet, and showed how his exquisite sensitiveness is a main factor in the wreck of his life . . . But best of all he loves Ophelia. How few Hamlets show this! They bully, they rave at, they ill-treat her, and curse her. They do not love her. . . This was Mr. Irving's finest acting scene, assisted as it was by an Ophelia as full of sensibility as himself. . . Hamlet's excitement stops the play long before the King is "frighted with false fire." The curtain drops, the courtiers crowd round the prostrate Prince, who crawls nearer and nearer to the steps of the throne, in order to throw his insults in his uncle's face. The effect of leaping on the empty throne was as fine as ever, but far finer than before the "subsidence of emotion" in the murder scene, where the fierceness of invective and satire were never shown with keener force or more refined polish.

For the other side of the coin we have several thrusts from the pen of William Archer:

In Hamlet, if we agree to add ten years or so to the age probably intended by Shakespeare, the careworn melancholy of Mr. Irving's countenance is perfectly suited to the character.

*   *   *   *

Mr. Irving is, of all distinguished actors, the least inspired. He never carries us away on the wings of his passion or his pathos, to set us down again after a little, wondering through what regions of terror or of beauty we have in the meantime been wafted. . . For my own part, I can remember to have been thus lifted out of myself by Salvini and [Joseph] Jefferson, by Sarah Bernhardt and Delannay, often by Mrs. Kendal, once or twice by Edwin Booth, but never, absolutely never by Mr. Irving. I am not, however, stating a mere personal impression; I speak from a close study of Mr. Irving's audiences.

Edmund Kean read Shakespeare by flashes of lightning: Mr. Irving reads him by the student's midnight oil.

(London 1883): *Henry Irving, Actor and Manager*

That Irving had grave physical handicaps to contend with is universally

Ellen Terry playing Ophelia to Irving's Hamlet (1879)

Irving as sketched by Fred Barnard in his dressing room in 1874

admitted. He never quite succeeded in freeing himself from certain provincial accents. His gait was awkward, even grotesque. Does this sound like a good Hamlet? Yet by high intellect and scrupulous attention to his art Irving became the accepted leader of the theatrical profession in England, a position similar to that held by Booth in America.

An account of Irving's Hamlet speaks well of Booth's earlier London appearance and paints a good picture of Act I, Scene 2:

> No one has quite succeeded in showing *how Hamlet would have played it* [the role of Hamlet]. And this is what Irving does. It is some years since Edwin Booth, who most nearly approached this natural and touching conception, was in England. . . That he is the best or at least the truest Hamlet, except Irving, we have, however, no doubt. He is so unequal an actor that his other performances give no indication of the grace, the intellect, poignant *nature* of his Hamlet; and the highest praise that can be accorded to Irving is that to the princeliness, the ease, the gravity, the intellect, and the naturalness of Booth - all of which he possesses, though a little more deeply stamped with personal manner — he adds these two remarkably contrasted qualities: a sort of domestic sensibility of the calamities and perplexities by which Hamlet is inundated, and a wild poetry of aspect and of speech which till now — unless indeed by the old actors before our time — has not been even hinted except by painters.
>
> Hamlet enters in the suite of the King and Queen. His face is pale and melancholy. His black hair is tumbled in masses, gracefully, but without any appearance of prearrangement. . . He sits while the others stand, not apart, however, in isolation, but in the midst, in semidistraction. There is no obtrusion of himself. Yet if you unveiled the picture to one who had never seen *Hamlet,* he would know that the hero of the play must be this darkhaired, mournfully garbed youth, leaning on his elbow, motionless, unaffectedly sad, making no show of grief, but gazing, it would seem, half pensively, half cynically, not so much into vacancy as into the heart of some oppressing mystery of sorrow.
>
> E. R. Russell (London 1875): *Irving as Hamlet*

Part of Irving's success lay in the sumptuous staging that he gave his plays and the fine talents of the fellow players with whom he surrounded himself. His productions at the Lyceum were studiously correct to the point of the smallest detail. Here he carried realism in the theatre to that perfectly pictorial taste in art which was the expression of his era. As electricity was utilized to focus attention upon actors free to wander in the deepest recesses of a new world of illusion, the aprons of stages receded. In his costuming the trimming of fur and the design of the metal sword-belt offered a slight suggestion of the Hamlet of history. Even Archer

Irving in the Ghost Scene (1874)

later admitted that no one could doubt that Irving's influence on the drama in England had been for the good.

Tommaso Salvini, the Italian actor, saw Irving's performance in 1875, His autobiography reveals his experience and his determination to attempt the role:

> I arrived at the theatre a little too late, so that I missed the scene of *Hamlet* in presence of the ghost of his father—the scene which in my judgment contains the clue to that strange character, and from which all the synthetic ideas of *Hamlet* are developed. I was in time to hear only the last words of the oath of secrecy. I was struck by the perfection of the stage setting. There was a perfect imitation of the effect of moonlight, which at the proper times flooded the stage with its rays or left it in darkness. Every detail was excellently and exactly reproduced. The scene was shifted, and Hamlet began his allusions, his sallies of sarcasm, his sententious sayings, his points of satire with the courtiers who sought to study and to penetrate the sentiments of the young prince. In this scene Irving was simply sublime. His mobile face mirrored his thoughts. The sublime penetration of his phrases, so perfect in shading and incisiveness, showed him to be a master of art. I do not believe there is an actor who can stand beside him in this respect, and I was so much impressed by it, that at the end of the second act I said to myself, "I will not play Hamlet! Mapleson can say what he likes, but I will not play it"; and I said it with the fullest resolution.
>
> In the monologue, "To be, or not to be," Irving was admirable; in the scene with Ophelia he was deserving of the highest praise; in that of the Players he was moving, and in all this part of the play he appeared to my eyes to be the most perfect interpreter of that eccentric character. But further on it was not so, and for the sake of art I regretted it. From the time when the passion assumes a deeper hue, and reason moderates impulses which are forcibly curbed, Irving seemed to me to show mannerism, and to be lacking in power, and strained; and it is not in him alone that I find this fault, but in nearly all foreign actors. There seems to be a limit of passion within which they remain true in their rendering of nature; but beyond that limit they become transformed and take on conventionality in their intonations, exaggeration in their gestures, and mannerism in their bearing. I left my box saying to myself, "I too can do *Hamlet, and I will try it!*"

Of Irving's Hamlet in particular it may be said that it was carefully conceived and notable in its essential humanness, especially in its tenderness toward Ophelia. Critics praised the expressive mobility of Irving's face and a voice most effective in its lower register. His jumping upon the empty throne at the conclusion of the Play Scene at once astonished and delighted.

Booth admired Irving. During a brief Othello-Iago association in London, Booth said, "At the Lyceum one sees the perfection of stage discipline, and in Mr. Irving the perfection of stage patience."

A contemporary comment on the 1878 Hamlet can be found in *The Edinburgh Courant:*

> The character begins to be regarded not merely as acting but as a poetic interpretation. It would attain much of its effect in mere reading without the advantage of stage accessories. For an artist whose elocution is so fastidiously and often absurdly criticised, Mr. Irving accomplishes marvels with his voice. It has no rival for the scope and variety of original meaning it can express. . . In rapid contrast of expression he has a power which has been perfected by the severest culture. . . Hamlet will be thought by many to remain Mr. Irving's finest role, because it evokes the greatest breadth of dramatic genius in him.

And in *The Theatre:*

> Free from the bonds of tradition, Mr. Irving presents us with a *human* Hamlet, and the realism he imparts to his acting rather intensifies than diminishes the halo of poetry which surrounds the character.
>
> The manner in which the tragedy is put on calls for very high praise. . . In two scenes the Lyceum artist may be said to have surpassed himself. The first is that in which the supernatural revelation is made. The ghost. . . standing among a number of massive rocks, proceeds to speak. The soft light of the moon falls upon the spectral figure; not a sound from below can be heard, and the first faint flushes of the dawn are stealing over the immense expanse of water before us. The weird grandeur of the scene can hardly be appreciated from description. Equally striking in its way is that of the burial of Ophelia. The churchyard is on a hill near the palace, and as night comes on the funeral procession winds slowly up the ascent. Never before have the "maimed rites" been so exactly and impressively performed. The scene of the battlements at Elsinor, with the illuminated windows of the palace in the background, and the star alluded to by Bernardo glistening in the northern sky, is also very effective. . . The scenery, like every other accessory, aids the imagination of the spectator instead of disturbing it.

In 1895, ten years before Irving's death and his burial in Westminster Abbey, Queen Victoria conferred upon the actor-manager the honor of knighthood, establishing a precedent that met with the wholehearted approval of the nation.

X

THE GREAT ITALIAN

Tommaso Salvini
1828-1915

IT IS PROPER to include among the Hamlets selected for this book at least one actor for whom English was not his native tongue. Fechter spoke with an accent, but Tommaso Salvini spoke only Italian. His success in the countries where the language of Shakespeare is held close to idolatry is, therefore, the more remarkable and a tribute to his genius as an actor. For Salvini *was* a genius. So completely did he immerse himself in his roles that he found it impossible to recuperate sufficiently for consecutive performances. There are no record "runs" set down for him as a theatrical achievement, only the record of audiences brought under the spell of a great actor. As a man, Salvini richly deserved that highest badge of genius—simplicity of heart, unspoiled by honors and the adulation of his followers.

Recognized at nineteen as a tragic actor of great promise (his parents were of the theatre, and he had made his debut at the age of fourteen), young Salvini forsook the stage to ally himself with his countrymen in the wars of Italian liberation. After the courageous, but futile, defense of Rome against the French, he was taken prisoner, to be commended later for his services by Garibaldi. It was but a brief interval in a long and honored stage career.

Immediately after his release from prison he embarked with mounting enthusiasm upon the study of Shakespeare. Then came performances in the theatres of Italy. "Nobody can play Hamlet but you," said his illustrious teacher, Gustavo Modena. The first of many extended tours took him to South America, where he was extolled and feted as no foreign actor had

Tommaso Salvini

ever been. In 1873 he journeyed to New York, and on four other occasions paid visits to the United States. Salvini liked America. He said that the vigor of its climate made him understand the energy and vitality of its people. There also were tours in England and performances in most of the Continental capitals, and then retirement before age might mar his power.

William Winter considered Salvini's American premiere a complete failure:

> We met in his dressing-room immediately after he had given his first performance in America of *Hamlet* [October 2, 1873]. The late Maurice Grau, then his manager, made us acquainted with each other, and we exchanged greetings. The man whom I saw (he had not yet laid aside the black-velvet stage-dress of the Melancholy Dane) looked like a gladiator. His performance, although mechanically efficient and worthy of a thoroughly practical actor, had been a complete failure, as it continued to be.
>
> He did not make Hamlet lovable, nor, except in the moment of his death, pathetic. . . A man more competent than Salvini's Hamlet to conduct all his affairs to a successful conclusion has never been shown upon our stage.
> (Moffat, Yard & Co. 1911): *Shakespeare on the Stage*

In England, however, where his Hamlet was performed at the Drury Lane in London on May 31, 1875, Salvini found a champion in the person of George Henry Lewes:

> Nevertheless I think of all the Hamlets I have seen, Salvini's is the least disappointing. Of all that I have seen, it has the greatest excellences. . . The scene with Ophelia was a revelation. Instead of roaring and scolding at her like other actors, with a fierce rudeness which is all the more incomprehensible that they do not represent Hamlet as mad, Salvini is strange, enigmatical, but always tender. . . The growing intensity of emotion during the play-scene culminates in a great outburst of triumphant rage as he wildly flings into the air the leaves of the manuscript he has been biting, a second before, and falls exhausted on Horatio's neck.
>
> No more pathetic death has been seen on the stage. Among its many fine touches there was the subtle invention of making the dying Hamlet draw down the head of Horatio to kiss him before sinking into silence:, which reminds one of the 'Kiss me, Hardy', of the dying Nelson. And this affecting motive was represented by an action as novel as it was truthful — namely, the uncertain hand blindly searching for the dear head, and then faintly closing on it with a sort of final adieu.
> (London 1875): *On Actors and the Art of Acting*

If Salvini is not to be numbered among the great Hamlets of history, it will be apparent for two reasons. In physique he was no more suited to the role than Edwin Forrest, and the greatness of his Othello overshadowed other interpretations. This was particularly true in the United States, where to see Salvini as Othello became a necessary part of one's experience in the theatre. Salvini, with a recognition of how the public visualized the Prince of Denmark, understood its preference to see him cast otherwise. This fact may account for the scarcity of photographs of him as Hamlet. Yet he liked the part, played it before enthusiastic audiences in his own country, on the Continent and in England, and brought to it the result of eager study and the magic of his art.

Salvini himself was fully aware of the light in which his Hamlet was regarded:

> In the eyes of the public my form seemed too colossal for Hamlet. The adipose, lymphatic, and asthmatic thinker of Shakespeare must change himself, according to the popular imagination, into a slender, romantic, and nervous figure; and although my Hamlet was judged more than flatteringly by the most authoritative critics, and by the first dramatic artist of that day, it will always take rank after my Othello.

(London 1893): *Leaves from the Autobiography of Tommaso Salvini*

Though Hamlet was not the perfect role for Salvini, and his interpretation divided the critics, praise did not come from mere blind veneration. In the presence of Ophelia he gave his Hamlet a very special quality of tenderness. To him the soliloquies were the poetry of the mind, and he made them seem spontaneous. Particularly was he admired for the climax to which he brought the play before the King, and the groping of the hands for his friend Horatio in the Death Scene.

Here is one American critic who took Salvini's Hamlet seriously:

> And he is not one who has what the French call *de beaux moments,* separated and made more conspicuous, as were Kean's, by scenes of comparative weakness; each of his characterizations is a complete and flawless whole, maintaining a level of highest art between the bursts of passionate inspiration.
>
> The part of Hamlet reveals the purely intellectual and poetic side of Salvini's genius, and is therefore, to my mind, among all his creations, the noblest and loftiest. "Salvini possesses," says the "Figaro," "the supreme qualities without which any actor who presumes to play Hamlet succumbs, miserably crushed under the weight of his own audacity. His grand and subtle elocution, and the profound intelligence which enables him to discern and fathom every feature of this colossal role, carry him to the loftiest regions of his art.". . .

Salvini makes him [Hamlet] a thinker. . . not a philosopher, but a poet. His delivery of the great soliloquy "To be or not to be," is that of a poet who thinks aloud; he neither recites nor declaims the words—he is apparently sincerely contemplating suicide, and deliberately weighing its promises and its terrors. Nothing could be more spontaneous, more natural, and more exquisitely beautiful.

The words "Al Chiostro!" [in the Ophelia Scene] are whispered, almost sighed forth, with unexampled tenderness and compassion. By his sincerity of belief in his own unworthiness he excites our sympathy for himself scarcely less than for her.

Salvini has a peculiar manner of repeating a simile. . . He pauses for an instant upon the conjunction, as if seeking the image exactly to correspond with the idea, and then delivers it with all the vivacity of a fresh inspiration. The airy grace of his action, which interprets his words to those who cannot understand his language, is strikingly apparent throughout the play. When Horatio relates the visitation of the Ghost, Salvini's gesture with which he accompanies the word "Armato?"—waving his hands from head to feet—is as eloquently descriptive of the mailed figure as Shakespeare's lines.

(1881, Vol. I, p. 110): *The Century Magazine*

His Ghost is commended by another critic:

His Hamlet was quite unsatisfactory to American audiences, and was seldom given in this country; but his performance of the Ghost far surpassed every other that our stage has known.

Henry Austin Clapp (Houghton, Mifflin 1902):
Reminiscences of a Dramatic Critic

Many have played Hamlet in a tongue that was not Shakespeare's, but none have excelled Salvini in the measure of their success in playing great roles before English-speaking audiences.

XI

A GRACIOUS PRINCE

Sir Johnston Forbes-Robertson
1853-1937

WHILE SALVINI COULD scarcely be said to look like Hamlet, Sir Johnston Forbes-Robertson most certainly did. Like Edwin Booth, Forbes-Robertson was an actor blessed by nature to be Hamlet. And to be a great Hamlet one not only must talk like a prince and walk like a prince, but also have that quality of soul which is in the prince that Shakespeare drew. There was grace and beauty in the hands of Forbes-Robertson, and in his face an intellect and nobility that a sculptor would idealize.

Those who had watched his development under the tutelage of Samuel Phelps and in Henry Irving's company felt instinctively that some day Forbes-Robertson would appear as Hamlet. London audiences realized with fervor in the season of 1897 that another Hamlet had arrived. He was in his forty-fourth year, late in time. And yet without that sumptuous quality of production that was Irving's and often with mediocre support, he illustriously identified himself with the role on both sides of the Atlantic.

During his reign as drama critic of *The Saturday Review,* George Bernard Shaw was an enthusiast for the Hamlet of Forbes-Robertson and, as the following comment shows, scarcely an admirer of Irving:

> The Forbes-Robertson *Hamlet* at the Lyceum is, very unexpectedly at that address, really not at all unlike Shakespeare's play of the same name.
>
> Mr. Forbes-Robertson takes the part quite easily and spontaneously. There is none of the strange Lyceum intensity which comes from the perpetual struggle between Sir Henry Irving and Shakespeare. The lines help Mr. Forbes-Robertson instead of getting in his way at every turn, because he wants to play Hamlet, and not slip into his inky cloak a changeling of quite another race.

104

Forbes-Robertson at the close of his career

Mr. Forbes-Robertson's own performance has a continuous charm, interest and variety which are the result, not only of his well-known familiar grace and accomplishment as an actor, but of a genuine delight—the rarest thing on our stage—in Shakespeare's art, and a natural familiarity with the plane of his imagination. He does not superstitiously worship William; he enjoys him and understands his methods of expression. Instead of cutting every line that can possibly be spared, he retains every gem, in his own part or anyone else's, that he can make time for in a spiritedly brisk performance lasting three hours and a half with very short intervals. He does not utter half a line; then stop to act; then go on with another half line; and then stop to act again, with the clock running away with Shakespeare's chances all the time. . . Not for a moment is he solemnly conscious of Shakespeare's reputation, or of Hamlet's momentousness in literary history: on the contrary, he delivers us from all these boredoms instead of heaping them on us.

October 2, 1897

Herman Merivale, on the other hand, links the new Hamlet with that of Fechter and Irving:

In Fechter's hands, somehow, even the philosophy seemed subservient to the action, and the stirring story never stood still for a minute. He was the best of all the impulsive Hamlets, as Forbes-Robertson ranks high among the intellectual ones, in the same category as Irving.

(November 1, 1897): The Theatre

In view of the recent stress on "runs" of Hamlet, Shaw's remarks toward the close of Forbes-Robertson's hundred-night engagement are of special interest:

Public feeling has been much harrowed this week by the accounts from America of the 144 hours' bicycle race; but what are the horrors of such an exhibition compared to those of the hundred nights run of *Hamlet!* . . . The performers had passed through the stage of acute mania, and were for the most part sleep-walking in a sort of dazed blank-verse dream. . . There was no act which did not contain at least one scene finely and movingly played; indeed some of the troubled passages gained in verisimilitude by the tormented condition of the actor. But *Hamlet* is a very long play; and it only seems a short one when the high-mettled comedy with which is is interpolated from beginning to end leaps out with all the lightness and spring of its wonderful loftiness of temper. This was the secret of the delighted surprise with which the public, when the run began, found that *Hamlet,* far from being a funereally classic bore, was full of a celestial gaiety and fascination.

December 18, 1897

Forbes-Robertson's Hamlet still haunts the memory of those who saw him, because he satisfied the eye, the discourse of his voice was like music

Forbes-Roberston
From the photograph by W. & D. Downey, London

to the ear, and the heart stirred before the presence of a gracious prince. He was a prince who could delight in his humorous banter with a grave-digger, while one felt the knife in the treatment of those friends whom he did not trust. As he played that most controversial scene with Ophelia, Forbes-Robertson, by his tenderness, and a restraint very near to the breaking-point, made completely convincing the fact that he had loved her.

It was this moment that prompted the critic of *The Boston Herald* to observe:

> Perhaps his best scene of all was that with Ophelia, where his power of self-control and suppressed feeling of love is a marvel of stage work.

(January 22, 1907)

Forbes-Robertson's madcap gaiety at the end of the play he had presented in the Court and his jesting gibes with Polonius were flashes of the Hamlet as he must certainly have been before the death of the father he had revered. And the conclusion of his performance was unforgettable; he conveyed no stark agony of realism, but instead an exaltation in the presence of death. When warlike Fortinbras appeared, peace had already descended, the triumphant peace of "flights of angels."

Clement Scott had the highest praise for the actor's interpretation:

> His voice, capable of every tone and modulation, is priceless. . . He does not attempt to make himself fanciful and pretty.
>
> What then. . . were the salient features of the newest of all new Hamlets? We should say two things. First, his consummate good breeding, united with frankness of nature and lovableness of disposition. Secondly, a mind sensitive to religious impression.
>
> We have never seen a Hamlet before who has in him such a subtle element of fun or such an appreciation of the whimsical. . . There are frequent evidences of this buoyancy of nature united to a supreme courtesy of manner.
>
> Most Hamlets approach this scene [Graveyard] like mutes, and preach out their sentiment as if they were in a pulpit. Not so Forbes-Robertson. His banter with the First Gravedigger is in the very lightest vein, and without a doubt these constant waves of brightness and sunshine are of extreme value to the spectator. . . The scene between Hamlet and Laertes at the grave was one of the best acted and most vigorous moments of the play. Here Hamlet awoke from the dreamer into the man of action; and the torrent of "rant," which was not rant at all, but the natural relief to an imprisoned nature, brought down the house.

(London 1900): *Some Notable Hamlets*

Though a painter of recognized merit, Forbes-Robertson did not allow his taste for color and design to interfere with his conception of a costume

Forbes-Robertson
From the original plate made in 1897 by W. & D. Downey, London

for Hamlet that was marked by great simplicity. He retained the metal chain and belt, but indulged in no decorative distractions of any kind. The staging followed the massive realism of his immediate predecessors.

Laying aside the robes of Hamlet at Harvard University in his sixty-fourth year to retire from the stage, Forbes-Robertson confessed with a plaintive sigh of relief that he had always found the role arduous and demanding. Only on two occasions, in morning performances requested by the members of his profession, could he recall being at ease in the part. He was not sure that he possessed the actor's temperament.

But let the actor speak for himself:

It was mainly due to the encouragement of Irving and Miss Terry that I ventured on a revival of "Hamlet".

When the announcements were being made I got a letter from George Bernard Shaw, whom I did not then even know by sight, beginning, "Dear Sir, I see that is is announced you are about to revive *Hamlet*. I suppose you think you are going to be very fine in the part, but let me tell you" — and then, covering four pages of foolscap, closely written, followed the kindliest, wisest advice as to the shoals and pitfalls attending such a step, and many valuable suggestions, some of which I carried out.

After saying farewell to my people, and many friends who had been in the audience, my friend Professor Baker in particular, I went down to my dressing room to take off Hamlet's robes for the last time. I had played the part many hundreds of times pretty regularly for over nineteen years, beginning at the mature age of forty-four, and ending in my sixty-fourth year. A revival of *Hamlet* had saved my financial position on many occasions. Over and over again both in England and America, when production of a new play had spelled failure, a revival of *Hamlet* had set me on my feet again. Yet I stripped myself of Hamlet's garb with no sort of regret, but rather with a great sense of relief, for not only was it my last appearance in a part which had cost me a vast amount of mental and physical strain, but the last of theatrical management, the gambling nature of which had always been abhorrent to me.

On looking back, it seems to me that I was far more nervous on the last performance of *Hamlet* than on the first. It is said that nervousness is a necessary attribute for an actor, and that he who does not suffer from it is rarely of much account in his art. It may be so, but all I can say is that so far as I am personally concerned, it has been nought but a shackling handicap. Never at any time have I gone on the stage without longing for the moment when the curtain would come down on the last act. Rarely, very rarely, have I enjoyed myself in acting. This cannot be the proper mental attitude for an actor, and I am persuaded, as I look back upon my career, that I was not temperamentally suited to my calling. For years I have fought hard

Entry of Fortinbras in final Scene at Lyceum Theatre, London
Forbes-Robertson's first performance of the role

Forbes-Robertson and his wife Gertrude Elliott

against this "ego," seldom would I reach that impersonal exhalation, so to speak, which it seems to me an actor should be able to attain. At rare intervals I have come by it in great passages of the Shakespeare tragedies, and notably when playing *Hamlet* on two occasions before audiences composed of my brother and sister players in New York.

Sir Johnston Forbes-Robertson (Little, Brown & Co. 1925):
A Player Under Three Reigns

In an article in a 1914 issue of *The Century Magazine,* toward the end of the actor's career, Richard Le Gallienne pays this tribute. It is eloquent in its description of the closing moment of the play:

To my thinking, the chief interest of all Forbes-Robertson's other parts is that they have "fed" his Hamlet. . . In Hamlet all his qualities converge . . . But of course the chief reason of that success is that nature meant Forbes-Robertson to play Hamlet.

Forbes-Robertson's acting is so imaginative, creating the scene about him as he plays, that one almost resents any stage-settings for him at all, however, learnedly accurate and beautifully painted.

And perhaps the most beautiful thing Forbes-Robertson's Hamlet does for us is that it commands our love for a great gentleman doing his gentlest and bravest and noblest with sad smile and a gay humor in not merely a complicated, wicked, absurd, and tiresome, but, also, a ghostly world.

Were one asked what aspects of Hamlet does Forbes-Robertson specially embody, I should say, in the first place, his princeliness, his ghostliness, then his cynical and occasionally madcap humor, as where, at the end of the Play Scene, he capers behind the throne in a terrible boyish glee. No actor that I have seen expresses so well that scholarly irony of the Renaissance permeating the whole play. His scene with Rosencrantz and Guildenstern and the recorders is masterly: the silken sternness of it, the fine hauteur, the half-appeal as of lost ideals still pleading with the vulgarity of life, the fine humor of its disillusion, and behind, as always, the heartbreak—the side of it which comes of the recognition of what it is to be a gentleman in such a world. . . . As a friend of mine graphically phrased it, "How he revives for us the splendor of the text!"

It is more than elocution, masterly elocution as it is, more than the superbly modulated voice: the power comes of spiritual springs swelling up beneath the voice—springs fed from those infinite sources which "lie beyond the reaches of our souls."

All my life I seem to have been asking my friends, those who valued the dearest, the kindest, the greatest, and the strongest in our strange human life, to come with me and see Forbes-Robertson die in *Hamlet*. I asked them because, as that strange young dead king sat upon his throne, there was something, whatever it meant—death, life, immortality, what you will—of a surpassing loneliness, something transfiguring the poor passing moment of trivial, brutal murder into a beauty to which it was quite natural that a stern Northern warrior, with his winged helmet, should bend the knee. I would not exchange anything I have ever read or seen for Forbes-Robertson as he sits there so still upon the throne of Denmark.

Forbes-Robertson is not only a great Shakespearean actor; he is also a great spiritual actor.

Forbes-Robertson, An Appreciation:
(*The Century Magazine* 1914)

In addition to Hamlet, Forbes-Robertson enjoyed other notable successes. If his career appears slighted in this brief essay, there is method in it. When an actor so perfectly identifies himself with a role as Forbes-Robertson did with Hamlet, what further need have we to obscure the view with irrelevant objects?

XII

ROMANTIC COMEDIAN

E. H. Sothern
1859-1933

IT IS NOW THE THEATRE IN AMERICA that is to show forth, in the person of E. H. Sothern, another worthy successor to this long line of Hamlets.

Edward H. Sothern was an actor's son. His father, E. A. Sothern, a peer among comedians, is justly famous as Lord Dundreary in *Our American Cousin,* the play performed at Ford's Theatre before President Lincoln that fatal night of April 14, 1865. Like many another professional father, he virtually forbade his son to follow in his footsteps. He saw no promise in the boy and knew well that the theatre is a wretched place for the mediocre actor, but he evidently failed to recognize the perseverance and courage that were to earn the younger Sothern high rank in the American theatre.

Sothern succeeded. After nearly two decades of seasons in comic and romantic parts his reputation was secure, yet no one dreamed of his assuming serious roles. He gave a good account of himself in *The Sunken Bell,* taken from the German of Gerhart Hauptmann, and the following season, early in the autumn of 1900, he appeared in New York as Hamlet. Although it was not altogether an occasion for cheering, audiences and critics alike were delighted by his Prince. There were faults in manner and voice, but the shrewder observers marked him for advancement.

The transition of the forty-year-old Sothern from romantic comedian to tragic actor is described by Lewis C. Strang:

> If I had been asked before the evening of December 22, 1899, to give a concise estimate of the professional standing of Edward H. Sothern, I should have written something like this: Mr. Sothern is a man of intelligence, an actor of worthy ambition and of laudable purpose. He has climbed steadily upward from the minor beginnings

GARDEN THEATRE

Madison Square Garden—Madison Avenue and Twenty-Seventh Street.

MADISON SQUARE GARDEN COMPANY, - - - - Proprietors
CHARLES FROHMAN, - - - - - - - - Manager
Also Manager of the Empire, Criterion, Garrick, Savoy and Madison Square Theatres, N. Y. City, and the DUKE OF YORK'S and VAUDEVILLE THEATRES, LONDON, ENG.

Every Evening at 7.45 P. M., Sharp.
Matinees New Year's Day and Saturday at 1.45 P. M., Sharp.

First Night Tuesday December 30, 1902

FOR FOUR WEEKS

E. H. SOTHERN

(Under the Management of DANIEL FROHMAN.)

THE TRAGEDY OF

HAMLET

PRINCE OF DENMARK.

By WILLIAM SHAKESPEARE.

DRAMATIS PERSONÆ.

CLAUDIUS, King of Denmark ....STEPHEN WRIGHT
HAMLET, son to the late and nephew to the present king.......E. H. SOTHERN
POLONIUS, Lord Chamberlain...................EDWIN VARREY
LAERTES, son to Polonius........................SYDNEY C. MATHER
HORATIO, friend to Hamlet ....HENRY J. CARVILL
OSRIC.................. ⎱ ⎰.............CECIL B. DE MILLE
ROSENCRANTZ.......⎰ Courtiers, ⎱...........RICHARD PITMAN
GUILDENSTERN.......⎰ ⎱...........GORDON JOHNSTONE
A PRIEST ....JOHN FINDLAY
MARCELLUS.......⎱ Officers, ⎰..........CHARLES VANN
BERNARDO . ..⎰ ⎱.........PERCIVAL T. MOORE
FRANCISCO, a soldier......................STEWART CAMERON
REYNALDO, servant to Polonius.................. PEDRO DE CORDOBA
FIRST PLAYER ....JOHN FINDLAY
SECOND PLAYER ....MALCOLM BRADLEY
FIRST GRAVEDIGGER....... ....ROWLAND BUCKSTONE
SECOND GRAVEDIGGER.................FREDERICK KAUFMAN
GHOST OF HAMLET'S FATHER......................WILLIAM HARRIS
FORTINBRAS, Prince of Norway........... ....CHARLES VANE
GERTRUDE, Queen of Denmark, and mother to Hamlet ......JENNIE EUSTACE
OPHELIA, daughter to Polonius ....CECILIA LOFTUS
PLAYER QUEEN.............. ....CHRYSTAL HERNE
Lords, Ladies, Officers, Soldiers, Messengers, Followers of Fortinbras, and other Attendants

SYNOPSIS OF SCENERY.

ACT I.—SCENE 1—Elsinore. A platform before the castle.
SCENE 2—A room of state in the castle.
SCENE 3—A room in Polonius's house.
SCENE 4—The platform.
SCENE 5—A more remote part
(Interval of ten minutes.)

ACT II.—SCENE—A room in the castle.
(Interval of two minutes.)

ACT III.—SCENE 1—A room in the castle.
SCENE 2—The Queen's closet.
(Interval of five minutes.)

ACT IV.—SCENE—A room of state in the castle.
(Interval of ten minutes.)

ACT V.—SCENE 1—A churchyard.
SCENE 2—A hall in the castle.
SCENE 3—A room of state in the castle.

Scenery by Unitt, of Daly's Theatre.
Costumes by M. Herrmann and I. Bloom, from designs by C. Karl.
Armor, L. and H. Nathan, of London.   Properties by Siedle.
Boots and Shoes by I. Miller.   Wigs by C. Meyer.
Supernumeraries rehearsed by William Parke.

Manager ....V. B. KENNEDY
Business Manager...SAMUEL FREEDMAN
Stage Manager..FRANCIS POWELL

PHOTO BY SCHLOSS

MR. SOTHERN as *Hamlet*

Playbill
E. H. Sothern's First Night, December 30, 1902

of *The Highest Bidder* to the major achievements of *The Prisoner of Zenda.* He has accomplished this much with dignity and without undue "booming." His reputation has been honestly won and is thoroughly deserved. In spite of a number of unfortunate and apparently settled mannerisms, and an obvious lack of sweeping breadth of style, he is a comedian of unusual finesse, of much subtlety, of sincerity, of great personal charm, and a romatic actor of grace, virility, and conviction.

On December 22, 1899, that estimate of Mr. Sothern was fair and reasonable; after December 22, however, it was valueless. For on that evening, when *The Sunken Bell,* Charles Henry Mettzer's English version of Gerhart Hauptmann's strange German play, *Die Versunkene Glocke,* was produced at the Hollis Street Theatre in Boston, a new E. H. Sothern came into being in the personality of Heinrich, the bell-founder.

The Sothern Hamlet was first shown in New York on September 17, 1900, and when one perceived the actor's astounding advance as a serious actor in the few months that had elapsed since his first performance of *The Sunken Bell,* one could do no less than accord him the tribute of both amazement and wonder. Mr. Sothern's Heinrich, as a sustained effort, was not at all as meritorious as his Hamlet. He acted Heinrich in flashes; his Hamlet, on the contrary, never fell to decided mediocrity, and more than once it whirled into passion and power. Mr. Sothern's chief technical fault was still his reading, but even this was far from bad. Certainly he never read any lines with a general excellence that approached his reading of Hamlet.

Without argument, one took the Sothern Hamlet seriously, which in itself was a great compliment to the actor's work.

Considered merely as an exhibition of acting, the shortcomings of Mr. Sothern's Hamlet were minor and unimportant—faults that continued practice and increased facility would, to a large extent, remedy.

One statement covered Mr. Sothern's impersonation most thoroughly. His Hamlet was decidedly a noteworthy performance, considered in detail; regarded as a whole, however, as a study of exposition and character, is was by no means wholly satisfactory. I could—anybody could—have picked flaws in Mr. Sothern's action from scene to scene, and these flaws were mainly to be found in his reading of the lines. Nevertheless, the Sothern Hamlet from scene to scene was powerful acting.

In pantomine, Mr. Sothern was notably good. He was satisfied with comparatively few introductions of new business. The scene of the first meeting with the ghost, especially Hamlet's fierce command to his friends to unhand him, was genuinely thrilling.

(L. C. Page & Co. 1902): *Famous Actors of the Day in America* (second series)

Sothern was always a hard worker. His fellow players recall how he

Julia Marlowe and E. H. Sothern

Marlowe and Sothern shortly after they began
twenty years of partnership in 1904

Hall
N.Y.

"HAMLET"

would often return to the stage after a performance to rehearse portions of his part that had failed to satisfy him. By mastering his weaknesses Sothern attained high competence, far higher than the faint praise the word suggests.

Yet William Winter does not appear to be a great enthusiast for the mature Sothern's Hamlet:

> It was, at its best, intelligent, conscientious, and sincere in spirit, picturesque in appearance, and methodical and evenly sustained in execution. Some of its defective points, apparent when it was first presented, were subsequently repaired—and that is true of every performance of the part which has endured at all—but it did not become authoritative and imposing. Filial tenderness and reverence were well expressed, as also, especially in the Closet Scene, were moral fervor and a withering scorn of evil-doing. In his later representations of Hamlet, when he apostrophized the Ghost, in the Closet Scene, and when he uttered Hamlet's dying words, Mr. Sothern was mournfully pathetic, striking a true note.
>
> In Mr. Sothern's earlier presentiments of *Hamlet* the indispensable passage, "Now might I do it, pat, now he is praying," was omitted; later it was restored. At first he used the advent of Fortinbras—customarily used on the European Continental Stage and always, whenever used, productive of tediousness—but later he discarded it. . . As a whole the performance, whether in its crudity at first or its maturity at last, was circumscribed within the conventional limits of stage utility. It was, however, largely attended and sometimes fervently praised. Every actor has his audience and Mr. Sothern's is a large one.
>
> (Moffat, Yard & Co. 1911): Shakespeare on the Stage

It was the company of Sothern and Marlowe that more than any other single influence revitalized Shakespeare for theatregoers throughout the United States. Julia Marlowe appeared with Sothern in 1904, beginning nearly twenty years of partnership and another instance, with good precedent, of a Hamlet's marrying his Ophelia. In Miss Marlowe, Sothern found a leading lady of rank, possessed with a voice of matchless beauty and a face that was lovely to behold. Year after year their tours in Shakespearean repertoire took them the length and breadth of the American continent. By the excellence of their productions, following literally the Booth precedent in staging and costuming, they enabled audiences to see Shakespeare well played.

H. K. M. in *The Boston Transcript* of December 23, 1911, finds the interpretation significant and explains why Sothern was so popular on the American stage:

The Play Scene designed for Sothern, 1904

Everywhere Sothern stresses the heroic, the virile, the determined —in short, the active.

He has many qualities—such as his crystal enunciation, the frictionless use of his rich voice, the fitness and restraint of much of his business. . . But his peculiar power with the American audiences, however, consists in his virility. . . to the average theatregoer he makes it [the role] glow with a truly American virtue.

Even after more than a score of years, and despite several actors notably, and even sensationally, successful in the role, Sothern's Hamlet was described by the critic of *The New York Daily Mail* as "the sanest, the most intelligent, the most scholarly and the most persuasive of them all." He went on to say:

It is not perhaps the most inspired. There are no moments when the emotional pull of his performance lifts you out of your seat. But there is a strong and steady movement to it and a fine sensitiveness for the poetry and meaning of the role that do quite as well.

Mr. Sothern, very evidently has concluded that his business is not to be E. H. Sothern but Hamlet, Prince of Denmark, as nearly as he can ascertain what the dramatist imagined Hamlet to be.

The scene in the Queen's closet, the breaking with Ophelia, and the scene with the players were all tense with the true spirit of tragedy.

Off the stage as well as on, Sothern evinced a certain air of distinction, of good breeding; he was to the manner born. His voice, at first far from a perfect instrument, was developed to the point of frictionless ease and richness. The mantle of Hamlet fell naturally upon his shoulders. Sothern had seen Booth's interpretation and was influenced by it. There also was something of the fire of Fechter in him. Without recourse to sensational new readings, Sothern made the poignant moments of the play genuinely thrilling. And yet it may well be that in the verdict of history the reputation of E. H. Sothern will rest principally on his contribution to the dramatic art rather than identification with a single role.

XIII

THE STATURE OF HAMLET

Walter Hampden
1879-1955

SOTHERN'S WAY WITH the play was somewhat conventional, but Walter Hampden brought to it a freshness in both interpretation and staging that impressed audiences profoundly.

When H. B. Irving, son of Sir Henry, was playing Hamlet in London in 1905, he was suddenly afflicted with loss of voice. The company might have been temporarily disbanded except for the recognized talents of a young American in the cast. Walter Hampden had but recently acted nearly seventy roles with Frank Benson's Shakespeareans. On the very briefest notice he showed that he knew what to do with the role of roles and played it with credit for a week. But it was more than a dozen years before he ventured seriously to undertake the part.

Sound schooling and training for the stage had preceded this London incident. A year at Harvard failed to arouse his enthusiasm, but in Paris his teachers felt that his developing talents could eventually have placed him at the Opéra or the Comédie Française. Hampden thought otherwise. He wanted to play the great stage creations of his native tongue.

Charles Rann Kennedy wrote *The Servant in the House* for Hampden. The Court Chamberlain refused permission for production in England, and on his decision hung Hampden's identification with the American stage. Henry Miller liked the young actor but was not sure of the play. However, when Hampden read it, he was captivated. The actor so completely became the Manson of the play that for some time he found it difficult to secure attention for other parts.

Toward the close of World War I, Hampden began his Hamlet

124

with much energy and effort by assembling prominent casts for special matinees in New York. He took it on tour in 1919, also playing Macbeth and Romeo, and adding Shylock in 1920. It was hard to find theatres for these matinees. Managers were doubtful; resident companies objected. In some towns not even pictures outside the theatres were tolerated. But Hampden persisted, and people began to recognize his talents. His Hamlet was the best on the American stage.

While drama critic for *The New York Evening Mail,* Burns Mantle reviewed the early Hamlet of Hampden on May 23, 1919:

> His Hamlet is also a more ingratiating youth, a less deeply melancholy prince than was the Sothern Hamlet when last we saw that scholarly and in most ways admirable performance.
>
> All the outstanding virtues of the Hampden Hamlet were first commended in the Forbes-Robertson Hamlet—the pervading spirit of gentleness, the modern note in the reading, the humor, the eloquent voice, the introspective analysis of the character.
>
> It honestly can be said, however, that the soul of Hamlet has never been entrusted to two finer guardians than these two, not since the day of Edwin Booth.

H. T. Parker was dramatic and music critic for *The Boston Transcript* for thirty years. He considered Hampden a worthy successor to Forbes-Robertson:

> They [the twentieth-century audience] ask an Hamlet of human semblance, quality, illusion. They ask that such a Hamlet be glamored by poetic speech and by poetized action. They ask that he keep place and pace in the vivid dramatic narrative which, basically again, is the play of *Hamlet* upon the stage. They received and applauded such a Hamlet from Forbes-Robertson. They now receive it yet again from Mr. Hampden.

Memories of Fechter were aroused for Philip Hale, the program annotator of the Boston Symphony Orchestra:

> Since the time of Fechter, no actor that we have seen has made so much of the great soliloquy beginning "O, what a rogue and peasant slave am I!". . . The soliloquies were admirably delivered, without the taint of conventional effects.
>
> On the whole a remarkably intelligent, engrossing, compelling performance; one that gives Mr. Hampden an honorable place by the great Hamlets of the past.
>
> (October 8, 1919): *The Boston Herald*

Alexander Woollcott would have it that Forbes-Robertson too soon was being forgotten:

> Mr. Hampden's performance as the sweet prince has been lauded to

the skies by some of his contemporaries. There has been, in some quarters, a disposition to hail him as the best Hamlet of our time. If, in this connection, the undefined phrase "our time" includes the period in which Forbes-Robertson's performance was visible in the American theatre, it would seem to this reviewer that some memories have been ungratefully short.

You could not possibly be bored by Walter Hampden's Hamlet, but probably your heart would not be greatly wrung by it either.

(March 17, 1920): *The New York Times*

J. Ranken Towse was a reviewer who began as an admirer of the Hamlet of Walter Hampden and never wavered in his opinion. His estimate of Booth and Forbes-Robertson is worth noting:

> Some of our younger dramatic chroniclers who have been lustily proclaiming Mr. John Barrymore as the best Hamlet of the last twenty-five years, must have forgotten Walter Hampden. It is a pity that they were not in the Montauk Theatre, of Brooklyn, last evening, if only for the purpose of refreshing their memories. They would have seen that disregarded player give a performance of the Dane not only far better than that with which he delighted the town in his earlier appearances, but if the present writer, who has seen every Hamlet of any distinction in the last sixty years, knows anything of what he is talking about—superior, as a whole if not in every detail, to any embodiment of that character since the best days of Edwin Booth.
>
> It has not the philosophic poise, formal elegance, or incisive diction of Booth, or the studied dignity and vibrant eloquence of Forbes-Robertson, but, on the other hand, it does possess a convincing naturalism which creates illusion and is extraordinarily effective.
>
> This is a human Hamlet if ever there was one. It has grace, dignity, fervor, pathos, intellectuality, and expressional power. It is a happy combination of the imaginative and the realistic, and last evening it held a great audience in unbroken thrall.

(December 15, 1922): *The New York Evening Post*

The modern tendencies in stage design were fully realized for Hampden by Claude Bragdon. For some time the photographic had been giving ground to the principles of dramatizing the mood of a play by artistic spacing and lighting. Hamlet's costume had already become simple, and Hamlet himself was finally permitted to move against an uncluttered background.

Walter Hampden played Hamlet more than 900 times. Next to his Cyrano it was his most successful role. Unlike the Hamlet of Sothern, which tended to deteriorate through over elaboration, or that of Forbes-Robertson, which remained virtually unchanged through the years, Hampden's Prince improved with age. It was at its best when the actor was between forty-five and fifty. With constant consideration for the value of each detail in the part, Hampden eliminated unessentials and added portions of the text that had long fallen into disuse. His Hamlet had a natural quality, behind which lurked the intellectual. It was an interpretation that possessed stature.

Two major critics, in appraising Hampden's performance in later years, were not entirely blinded by the sudden brilliance of John Barrymore in the role:

> If he lacks the magnetic glamour of the lovely though less studious and profound Mr. Barrymore, he is still a gratifying object to those who like their Hamlets undiluted..
>
> Percy Hammond (October 12, 1925):
> *The New York Herald Tribune*

> Mr. Hampden's conception of the part is open to fussy criticism. It is youthless and unreasonably weary; the lighting as well as Mr. Hampden's expression make it appear theatrically pallid in the opening scenes. It lacks the full range between impersonal self-pity and unmeasured anger. But it seldom comes between the character of Hamlet and the audience. All we need is the expression of Hamlet. Mr. Hampden achieves more beautifully than many actors who have set the character aflame.
>
> Brooks Atkinson (January 5, 1928): *The New York Times*

Well-deserved honors came to Walter Hampden. His voice, rich in tone and delightful in clarity of utterance, won for him a motion-picture Academy Award for excellence in diction. As successor to the lustrous Booth, Jefferson, and Drew, he was president of The Players at his death on June 11, 1955.

Hampden's approach to Hamlet was on a high plane indeed, but with the appearance of John Barrymore a rare kind of excitement entered the theatre.

For Dear Margaret Carrington—
with the greatest love and gratitude
from her offspring—

Old Pop Hamlet!

1923

XIV

A GLIMPSE OF GREATNESS

John Barrymore
1882-1942

JOHN BARRYMORE WANTED to be an artist; in fact he was employed for eighteen months in the art department of *The New York Evening Journal.* Strengthened by his conviction that "the indifferent painter usually starves," the youngest of a family illustrious in the theatre may have felt that somewhere he was destined for fame as an actor. The records of the "royal family" are too well known to necessitate repetition here.

Barrymore's Hamlet was by general election awarded a place among the great stage events after the turn of the century. He quit the role in London in his forty-fourth year after nine weeks of performances to devote himself to motion pictures. Few American actors have ventured their Hamlets before London audiences; Barrymore's was a triumph. During the ordeal of the opening night, in an effort to calm the nerves of his company, he strolled behind the curtain with a cigarette, soothed no doubt by a message that Bernard Shaw was "out front." Then, in unbroken file, came John Masefield, Lord Dunsany, Somerset Maughan, and others.

Indolent by his own admission, the young Barrymore made sporadic attempts in the theatre to ward off starvation. He also confessed to being a very bad actor. There were the vicissitudes of appearances with his sister Ethel, the San Francisco earthquake, an Australian tour with William Collier, motion pictures, and then, John Galsworthy's *Justice.* This first effort at serious drama aroused his fears to such a pitch that he hurried about the lobby, nervously pasting stickers over his name. There was, of course, no failure; instead, one season after another of dramatic successes. Barrymore thought that *The Jest,* in which he starred with his

John Barrymore's autographed photograph to Margaret Carrington, *"With the greatest love and gratitude from her offspring Old Pop Hamlet"*

John Barrymore, 1922   Barrymore with John S. O'Brien as Polonius

brother, Lionel, might run for two or three weeks. How wrong he was! The public could never get enough of it, and a season and a half was deliberately terminated to prepare for *Richard III.*

Barrymore became the most brilliant member of his profession. He knew that eventually Hamlet would be demanded of him. His first preparation for the role came in walks through the woods about White Sulphur Springs, Virginia. He liked the part, which was to become the only one "always fresh to me." His New York debut at the Sam H. Harris Theatre on November 16, 1922, created a furor, and his Hamlet broke Booth's record by one performance. Barrymore took the play on tour the following season, and then, after lengthy negotiations, to London, and retirement.

Alexander Woollcott's review of the opening in New York reads in part:

> Certainly here is no palimpsest of all the Hamlets that have tottered or waddled or stalked humorless past us in these later years, but a Hamlet reborn and one that, for all its skill and graphic artfulness, is so utterly free from all that is of the stage stagey. Issuing from his lips, the very soliloquies which have so often separated out from the rest of the play as set pieces of oratory seemed to have been spoken for the first time last evening, seemed to have been thought for the first time, and in the complete silence that was their audience's tribute to something genuine and alive they seemed for once just a lonely, unhappy man's thoughts walking in the silent darkness.
>
> He has played Hamlet and to the part to which all his own qualities and talents bade him go he has brought new gifts of voice and stature and understanding. It is the realest Hamlet we have known.
>
> (November 17, 1922): *The New York Herald*

His endowments and qualities for Hamlet were rich—what Woollcott called "such qualities of mind and mask as life gives sparingly a few times in a hundred years." His Hamlet was graceful in movement, perfect in accent, compelling in personality. But more than that, it had an electric quality that produced bodily sensations as one sat as a witness before the play. It was a Hamlet with a capacity for friendship, and at once a searing scorn in the presence of treachery; passionate and tender as it revealed the troubled heart.

In a dissenting opinion, Heywood Broun took exception to the actor's voice:

> The falling off from what would seem to us the Hamlet of a dream lay in Barrymore's diction. He has done marvels with his voice. In

Barrymore with Tyrone Power as Claudius

Robert Edmond Jones Play Scene set for Barrymore's production

fact he has done too much. In gaining what seems to us an almost absolute precision some of the emotion and eloquence which lie in occasional imperfection is gone. Tones which rasp the ear may tear at the heart. We not only felt that Barrymore was constantly correct but that he knew he was correct. There was at least the possibility of suspicion that his alma mater was not Wittenburg but Harvard. The tragedy of things that happen to finished young men is somehow a little less poignant. And then again this was a Hamlet so exceedingly shrewd and wise that it was difficult to believe in his failure.

(November 18, 1922): *The New York World*

This staging of Hamlet has at times been referred to as the Barrymore-Jones-Hopkins production, a title that suggests the nature of the modern theatre. Robert Edmund Jones designed the sets, and Arthur Hopkins was the producer. No such three-way emphasis appears in stage annals up to that time. A most controversial note was sounded in their representing the Ghost by an eerie, wavering light, with the voice emanating off stage—an unsatisfactory good intention at best. Barrymore's costume was as severely simple as any worn by a distinguished Hamlet.

Walter Pritchard Eaton, who directed the affairs of the drama at Yale University, gives his impressions of several Hamlets:

Booth had dynamic tragic power and a naturally brooding, melancholy disposition. Irving had less tragic power, but as no man of our age, he possessed the ability to suggest with uncanny effect a mind haunted, distraught. . . Yet the Barrymore-Jones-Hopkins production is worth seeing; as were most decidedly the Forbes-Robertson production, the Walter Hampden production, the E. H. Sothern production, and numerous lesser ones.

The poetry of the play, specifically exhibited in the verse, is what I best remember of Forbes-Robertson's performance, and what I least remember of Irving's. This ability to deliver blank verse is a conspicuous merit of Walter Hampden. It ought to be of Mr. Barrymore, but is not as yet.

(January 10, 1923): *The Freeman*

Late in 1923, before the company went on tour, Woollcott wrote:

Now we have both the profound thought and the troubled heart, and something has given the blending smoothness. Perhaps it is merely because *Hamlet* has become easy second nature to one who knows it better and is freed by the mere familiarity.

(December 1, 1923): *The New York Herald*

After the opening in Boston, H. T. Parker of *The Transcript* described the Closet Scene as "without parallel in a lifetime of play going." Captivated by Barrymore's performance, he went on:

For this Hamlet of John Barrymore, as it seemed to one spectator, thrilled and holden before it, is neither old-fashioned nor new-fashioned, of this theory and practice or of that. Rather, it is the Hamlet of an actor of imagination and resource, of penetrating mind and enkindled spirit, face to face with Shakespeare's personage, firmly, almost desperately, resolved to be honest with the character, honest with himself. . . The outcome is a Hamlet in which spiritual sensation succeeds spiritual sensation. . . from the prose, say, of the scene with the players, from the confusions of the scene with Ophelia, into the poetry and the beauty clarified of the scenes after the return. It is a Hamlet of burning intensities, and wire-strung sensibilities.

Of Barrymore' performance at the Haymarket Theatre, where he opened on Feb. 19, 1925, James Agate, critic of *The Times of London,* wrote:

> Mr. Barrymore's Hamlet draws fewer tears than Forbes-Robertson's, but it is nearer to Shakespeare's whole creation than any other I have seen. In fact, this *is* Hamlet, since you have but to scratch the god and the demon appears.
> The Play Scene was immensely fine, its climax being a miracle of virtuosity, and the Closet Scene was perfection. Much of the latter was spoken on Gertrude's breast, and the pathos was overpowering. And from here right on to the end I thought the performance magnificent. It gathered power, coherence, and cumulative effect; in short, we knew ourselves to be in the presence of a fine and powerful mind.
> (February 22, 1925): *The London Sunday Times*

One wonders whether the Prince of John Barrymore, this brightest of all Hamlet memories, can long remain visible through the arches of the years. Let treble woe fall ten times double on the head of Hollywood!

For the last seventeen years of his life the theatre-going public was deprived of his rare talents.

XV

RECORD HOLDER

Sir John Gielgud
1904

THE DEPARTURE OF JOHN BARRYMORE created a void in the theatre. For a dozen years the public was without a good *Hamlet* production. John Gielgud, after achieving critical and popular acclaim in London, arrived in New York, a worthy successor.

This talented actor, relative of Dame Ellen Terry, first played Hamlet at the Old Vic at the age of seventeen, and finally, before appearing at the Empire Theatre in New York on Oct. 8, 1936, he had completed a record run of 155 consecutive performances as the Prince. Gielgud's Hamlet was so popular that he had no difficulty in achieving a new American record, to follow it with a tour of five weeks. Only previous commitments forced him to cut short his travels and return to England.

From the pages of *The New York Times* we glean the comments of Brooks Atkinson on Gielgud's Hamlet:

> For this is no roaring, robustious Hamlet, lost in melancholy, but an appealing young man brimming over with grief. His suffering is that of a cultivated youth, whose affections are warm and whose honor is bright. Far from being a traditional Hamlet, beating the bass notes of some mighty lines, Mr. Gielgud speaks the lines with the quick spontaneity of a modern man. His emotions are keen. He looks on tragedy with the clarity of the mind's eye.
>
> What Mr. Gielgud's Hamlet lacks is a solid body of overpowering emotion, the command, power and storm of Elizabethan tragedy.
>
> But the sensitivity of Mr. Gielgud's personality, as it is revealed on the stage, the cultivation of his manners and the intellectual quality of his acting give him a closer resemblance to Shakespeare's Hamlet than anyone who has acted him since Forbes-Robertson.
>
> The touch of nature that makes the whole world kin is lacking in his performance. Although he probes the mind admirably, he is

John Gielgud, 1934   Hamlet with Polonius in London production

too shallow a vessel for the turbid rancor and scorn. He is all Hamlet, but not the whole of Hamlet, which is a tumultuous part for the stage.

In his review, Richard Watts Jr. of *The New York Herald Tribune* preferred Barrymore's Prince:

> My standard of excellence in a characterization of Hamlet is frankly Mr. Barrymore. His was, to my mind, not only the finest portrayal of the role I have ever seen but was also the most magnificent piece of acting within my memory. If I think that Mr. Gielgud's performance is somewhat less impressive, it is because he fails to capture the demoniacal humor and thrilling theatrical eloquence that Mr. Barrymore brought to the role. Unquestionably, there was a bitter, self-destroying sense of fun about Hamlet, and Mr. Gielgud makes him rather a humorless man. . . Every speech comes from him as if it had arisen from the depths of his embittered mind. The famous soliloquy is spoken, not with the fiery Barrymore eloquence but as if it were really a debate going on in the brain of the man; the careful result of his tortured contemplation. His Hamlet is not passionate, but it is brooding and neurotic.

It is a second-best Hamlet in the eyes of John Mason Brown, and one can detect a nostalgia for Forbes-Robertson:

> It will be Mr. Gielgud's voice in the future we shall hear lending its color to many of the nobler speeches. Such a voice, such diction, and such a gift for maintaining the melody of Shakespeare's verse even while keeping it edged from speech to speech with dramatic significance, is a new experience to those of us who since the twilight days of Forbes-Robertson have seen a small army of actors try their wings, and sometimes our patience, as Hamlet.
>
> If, in spite of a frequent brilliance, occasional superiorities and steady interest of Mr. Gielgud's Hamlet, his Prince still plays second-best to Mr. Barrymore's, one reason is that Mr. Gielgud's Hamlet lacks the consistency Mr. Barrymore brought to the part. Many of the details of his Hamlet are fine. Some are magnificent.
>
> One gladly overlooks the lapses in his interpretations.
>
> (October 9, 1936): *The New York Post*

Gielgud had scarcely settled in the Van Dyke dressings elected for his court of Elsinore when Leslie Howard, after a week at the Boston Opera House, appeared at the Imperial Theatre with his version of the play. The respective merits of these apparent rivals were quickly determined by critics and audiences alike. Ironically, the failure of Howard's Prince made assurance doubly sure for the success of its rival. A minority insisting on the greater appeal of the production and interpretation of Leslie Howard could not make itself heard above the din. At least there was some satisfaction for the Hollywood star in the support of good audiences on an extended tour. In the critical opinion of John Mason Brown it was doubtful if any distinguished player had ever attempted the part and acted it throughout with less distinction.

In an interview during his American tour, Gielgud gave it as his firm conviction that no actor should undertake Hamlet after reaching the age of thirty-four. He has held to this conviction. His great achievements in the theatre, both as actor and director, were rewarded with a knighthood in 1953.

XVI

THE UNCUT HAMLET

Maurice Evans
1901

GIELGUD'S DECISION TO ABANDON the role left American audiences with no Prince of Denmark. Great was the rejoicing when Maurice Evans introduced his uncut version of the play.

The choice of the profession of actor came less certainly to Evans than to Gielgud. From a boy singer and an interest in theatricals he entered the business of music publishing. But the pull of the stage was too strong. He, too, played Hamlet at the Old Vic, giving there his "uncut" version that was later to be so highly favored in New York.

Association with Katharine Cornell as Romeo and the Dauphin marked Evans as an actor of genuine talent, and the cheers that greeted the final curtain on his appearance as Richard II announced a Shakespearean of acknowledged eminence.

If the New York drama critics have placed, with some reservation, their stamp of approval on John Gielgud's Hamlet, they have surely waxed eloquent, even ecstatic, in their praise of the interpretation and production of Maurice Evans. His full-length presentation at the St. James Theatre restored the play to the original intentions and conceptions of its author, and many a playgoer remarked that he would never again be satisfied with a garbled *Hamlet.* It necessitated a long session in the theatre, yet one was astonishingly unconscious of the passage of time.

In their reviews of the premiere, Brooks Atkinson and Richard Watts Jr. bestowed praise on Evans' Hamlet and the directing of Margaret Webster:

> For the uncut *Hamlet* is a wild and whirling play of exalted sound and tragic grandeur, and Mr. Evans acts it as though it were

Maurice Evans
Maurice Evans in New York 1938-39.
Costume and Scenery by David Ffolkes

Act I, Scene 2; George Graham as Polonius, center; Henry Edwards as Claudius and Mady Christians as Gertrude. Evans is at far right

a new text that had not been clapper-clawed by generations of actors. Out of the prompt-book he and his director, Margaret Webster, have snatched it and put it onto the modern stage. It is compact with life. Apparently Shakespeare was a great writer, because he could put lusty parts into a turbulent play; and this long, fiery tale of murder, despair and revenge is the most vivid drama in town today.

It is a headlong play of vital scope in the ample text of the second quarto. That is the fresh spirit in which Mr. Evans takes it. He acts it at the top of his compass. On the negative side, he has abandoned the posturing, the school-book melancholy, the rigid acting situations and set speeches that tradition has imposed upon Hamlets, and he does not interpret the business fearfully. On the positive side, he acts a Hamlet of modern sensibilities who does not love words for their own sake but for their active meaning. This is a Hamlet of quick intellect who knows what is happening all through the play. He dominates by alertness. He is frank; and, above everything else, he is lucid.

Brooks Atkinson (October 13, 1938):
The New York Times

*   *   *   *   *

His [Evans'] Prince of Denmark is no hysterical, white-faced neurotic, but a passionate and vigorous man, accustomed to action as well as words, but caught up in a net of tangled events that brought out all the contradictions in his violent and sensitive nature.

Mr. Evans expressed in a curtain speech the hope that the current production might show people that "Hamlet" was a drama and not a study in dyspepsia.

It is, of course, one of the great qualities of Mr. Evans' acting that he can combine eloquence of speech with intelligence and soundness of characterization to an extent that makes him the most satisfying of Shakespearean actors. Here is assuredly the finest Hamlet that we have seen in our town since John Barrymore's classic portrayal of the role. Something of the savage, sardonic humor that went into Mr. Barrymore's performance is missing from the present characterization, as is some of the relish that went into a few of the individual speeches in the earlier presentation. On the other hand, it is probably a more consistent characterization. This is, as I have said, a vigorous, violent and masculine Hamlet, who is not overly bothered with psychopathic pallor. It is Hamlet the roisterer, the gay student of Wittenburg, as well as the scholar, the dreamer and the ironic philosopher. It is a Hamlet with a love of rhetoric and a high spiritual sensitivity, but also a Hamlet capable of plots and battle. And never is that superb eloquence omitted or let down.

Miss Margaret Webster's direction is vivid and imaginative. Mr. Evans's Hamlet is one of the great and satisfying events of the modern theatre.

Richard Watts Jr. (October 13, 1938):
The New York Herald-Tribune

The Play Scene

Evans with Katherine Locke as Ophelia

153

The skillful and intelligent direction of Miss Webster has rightly shared in the praises. It was apparent that nothing was said or done without having first been clearly thought out in advance. The players knew what they were about. Evans makes his Hamlet the kind of royal student that one would like to have known. His balance of the varying moods of the role is admirable.

John Mason Brown notes the creating of a new tradition:

> It takes a few minutes to become adjusted to Mr. Evans as Hamlet, even as it did to surrender to his Romeo. At first sight he seems to lack physical presence. During the initial court scene he is haunted inescapably by memories of John Barrymore's lean regality and Mr. Gielgud's fiery unhappiness. But soon thereafter he establishes himself triumphantly in the part. His Prince escapes detailed comparison with recent Hamlets by being a Hamlet that is very much Mr. Evans' own. It does not follow tradition; it creates a new and, if I may say so, very welcome one.
>
> (October 13, 1938): *The New York Post*

During Evans' second season in New York, critics Watts and Brown returned for a second appraisal of the Briton's Prince:

> It can now be said categorically that Maurice Evans' production of *Hamlet* is just as brilliant and exciting as all of us thought it was when we saw it for the first time last year. . . one of the great experiences of playgoing is offered once more in all its magificence.
>
> As for Mr. Evans's portrayal, it remains the ablest and most satisfying rendition of the epic role seen in New York since John Barrymore's historic performance. Again he makes the unhappy prince not a white-faced, hysterical neurotic, but a vigorous, virile man caught up in a net of circumstances that brought out all the bitterness and all the contradictions in his subtle character. Not since Mr. Barrymore has any Hamlet so captured the sardonic humor and the inherent capacity for gaiety in the man or the qualities of roistering fellowship that make comprehensible his student days at Wittenburg. If the Evans portrayal lacks some of the biting Barrymore brilliance, it seems to me, on the other hand, to possess a more even and consistent quality than his predecessor offered.
>
> Richard Watts Jr. (December 5, 1939):
> *The New York Herald Tribune*

* * * * *

The wonder is that Mr. Evans' Dane is really the superb creation it is. Mr. Evans cannot claim Mr. Barrymore's face and figure. He does not erupt into those uncertain moments of sheer brilliance Mr. Gielgud achieved. He is really a character actor faced in Hamlet with the challenge of playing a straight part. But so unmatched is his technique, so refreshing is his interpretation, so excitingly concerned is he with the excitements of the entire play, and so stunning is his

154

voice that, while many actors may have excelled him in this scene or that, no one in our time has done greater justice in the theatre to the whole Hamlet than has he.

John Mason Brown (December 5, 1939): *The New York Post*

In both the Gielgud and Evans productions one notes a distinct movement away from the stark severity of the dress and setting of their immediate predecessors. If Gielgud clung to the solemn black of the text, he made it seem less austere in knee-breeches. The three costumes assumed by Evans were scarcely literal in their sumptuous quality. Even so, they did not offend.

Actors grow into the part by long experience. Evans' second season in New York showed a maturing actor as the Prince. By December 20, 1939, he had played the role 200 times, and many more performances were to follow. He toured in his GI *Hamlet* during the war, but did not, however, use the uncut version. This fine actor has added much to the popular appeal of the role.

XVII

PLAYER OF POWER

Richard Burton
1925

YEARS WERE TO ELAPSE after the high standards that Maurice Evans brought to the play before a new star appeared. Hopes were high that in the talents of Richard Burton would be revealed a fresh Hamlet and one of great fascination.

Before he had reached the age of thirty, Old Vic audiences thrilled to the Hamlet of Richard Burton, the twelfth of thirteen children of a Welsh coal-miner's family. His rise to this peak of greatness had been little short of sensational. He has said of himself, "The idea of a Welsh miner's son going to Oxford University was ridiculous beyond the realm of possibility."

Recognized early as a lad of promise, Burton was fortunate in coming under the tutelage of an extraordinary man, who became his adopted father and whose name he assumed. Philip Henry Burton was drama coach and English master in a neighboring town. Up to the age of ten, the younger Burton had spoken only Welsh, and it was from his foster-father-teacher that he learned English in the King's tradition, and the controlled, yet effortless, projection of voice that was to become his greatest asset as an actor. A story is told of how his teacher took him to a high hill and made him speak Shakespearean lines as he moved farther away. "Make me hear it," he commanded, "but don't shout."

When he was sixteen, Richard Burton answered an ad of Emlyn Williams for an actor who could speak Welsh and look like twenty-two. He got the part, and the way to his professional career was open. The winning of a competitive scholarship brought him to Exeter College, Oxford, but the age requirement forced a delay in his entrance, during which time he scored a stage success in London. His one year at Oxford was primarily concerned with OUDS, the Oxford University Dramatic Society, then under the shrewd and talented eyes of Nevil Coghill. The play then in rehearsal was *Measure for Measure*, but all parts were already filled. Undaunted, he asked to understudy the lead. Burton is apt to get what he wants, and he got the part. He was not forgotten. Opportunities awaited him in the London theatre when his service with the Canadian Air Force was completed.

His first appearance on a New York stage came in 1950, when he was starred with John Gielgud and Pamela Brown in Christopher Frye's *The Lady's Not for Burning*, previously produced in London. It was in 1953 that he played many Shakesperean roles with the Old Vic, his Hamlet proving particularly noteworthy. After one of these performances, Sir Winston Churchill commented that it was as exciting and virile as anything he could remember. Moss Hart felt that actors like Burton were born once in fifty years and that "unlike most stars, whose magnetism disappears away from the footlights, Burton remains full size." Kenneth Tynan considered him "another Edmund Kean."

In light of Burton's approach to the role, the London Times reviews of the Old Vic company add a comment to his interpretation:

> The Old Vic company are a great deal happier on their own stage than they were with the same tragedy on the platform stage at Edinburgh. There they tried Elizabethan methods of presentation, aiming to project the play into our midst with acting that was not so much "miming" as "speech-making" or "costume recitation." We also are happier. We need no longer pretend to be Elizabethans. We can settle down to enjoy seeing the tragedy acted on a stage which may not produce the intimacy the Elizabethans knew but at least produces that measure of illusion we have come to expect.
>
> Mr. Richard Burton's playing of Hamlet in the new surroundings has become something altogether different. On the platform stage it was curiously without charm. That Hamlet seemed to be suffering acutely but rather sullenly and unsympathetically. The delivery of the soliloquies was the most powerful part of the performance. This Hamlet has charm which, for all of its melancholy, is not to be resisted, and the power still felt in the soliloquies is felt now everywhere.
>
> We are aware of it alike in the sullen reserve of his early exchanges with the king, in the shock of the ghost's revelations, in the tenderness which is not to be altogether suppressed in his ambiguous treatment of Ophelia, in the sudden gaiety with which he greets the players, in the fierce animation with which he conducts the play scene; in short, at every fascinating turn of a performance which is as satisfying as any that memory can recall for a great many years. The worst thing to be said in dispraise of its technical accomplishment is that when Burton raises his voice louder and louder in declamation the last note is apt to be so loud that it becomes inaudible.

Richard Burton as Hamlet in the New York performance

Burton with George Rose as the Gravedigger (left) and John Cullum as Laertes

It was not until April 9, 1964, that his *Hamlet,* under the direction of Sir John Gielgud, was first seen by New York audiences. There were those who found fault with Burton's interpretation, but to most it was as good a Hamlet as had been seen in this generation. A limited engagement at the Lunt-Fontanne Theater was extended well into midsummr. So, too, there were those who disliked the costuming or, shall we say, the lack of costuming. You came in the garb you wore in the last rehearsal. It is a tribute both to the acting and to the play itself that this seeming handicap could be overcome. Burton's voice and posture caught the attention of all. His great mentor had taught him the value of standing still, for it is this that focuses interest.

Reviewing Burton's performance in *The New York Times,* Howard Taubman, successor to Brooks Atkinson, clearly was impressed by the Welsh actor's intepretation of the Prince:

> Richard Burton dominates the drama, as Hamlet should. For his is a performance of electrical power and sweeping virility. But it does not burst the bounds of the framework set for it by John Gielgud's staging. It is not so much larger than life that it overcomes the rest of the company. Nor does it demand attention so fiercely for itself that the shape and poetry of the play are lost to the audience.
>
> Mr. Gielgud's own Hamlet years ago was much different—more sinuous and refined. It is his merit that he has found a new way to look at the play to be in keeping with Mr. Burton's style and view of the role. This is no melancholy Hamlet, no psychological or "Oedipal" Hamlet, no effete or lackluster Hamlet.
>
> It is clear early on that Mr. Burton means to play Hamlet with all the stops out—when power is wanted. He is aware of the risk of seeming to rant. For it is he who warns that the players must not tear a passion to tatters. But he is unafraid—and he is right.
>
> I do not recall a Hamlet of such tempestuous manliness. In the first two soliloquies Mr. Burton does not hestitate to cry out as if his very soul were in torment, and the thunderous, wrenching climaxes do not ring false. But he reads the "To be or not to be" soliloquy with subdued anguish, like a man communing with himself. Then in the scene that follows with Ophelia he begins by being ineffably tender, but when he rails at her to get to a nunnery, his rage bespeaks his hatred for himself as well as for a base world.
>
> Mr. Burton's Hamlet is full of pride and wit and mettle. He is warm and forthright with Horatio. As he listens to Polonius's windy craftiness, a look of shrewd contempt hoods his eyes. He trades quips with the First Gravedigger with gusto.

Mr. Burton's voice is not mellifluous like those of a few highly cultivated classic actors. It has a hearty ring and a rough edge, attributes that suit his interpretation. He does not, however, scant the poetry. He has a fine sense of rythm. It is very much his own, with a flair for accenting words and phrases in unexpected ways. But the result, while personal, does no violence to sound or sense.

Walter Kerr, writing in The *New York Herald Tribune,* found a major flaw in Burton's portrayal:

Richard Burton is one of the most magnificently equipped actors living, and in John Gielgud's rehearsal-clothes production of *Hamlet* he places on open display not only all of his own reverberating resources—a face that is illuminated in repose a voice that seems to prove that sound spirals outward, an intelligence that hears wit when wit is trying to steal by tiptoe—but also all of the myriad qualities which the man Hamlet requires. All except one.. Mr. Burton is without feeling.

I do not know why emotion—intimated or actual, suppressed or open—has escaped him so entirely in this role which breeds maggots of emotion. Mr. Burton has always been a somewhat abstracted actor, a man whose pale, cool eyes could detach themselves from whatever was ravaging his mind for a moment abating the ferocity, or even the meaning, of his performance. But in *Hamlet,* as we are now offered it at the Lunt-Fontanne, we hear the sound of the hammering without seeing any splinters fly up.

The absence of genuinely felt heat—the kind of heat that will actually inform a raging soliloquy instead of reporting it at an adopted pitch—splits the performance, and perhaps even the production, in two. The wit is there, the intelligence stands clear. With no more than a faint retard the actor can imply that Claudius is a posturer. By dropping each of four words a tone at a time, as though they were worthless coins being dropped into a canyon, he can judge his mother ("O most pernicious woman") so finally that for her Judgment Day will be an entirely superfluous occasion.

And he can convey, better than anyone I have seen do, the kind of savage glee that sometimes comes of knowledge, even horrifying knowledge. Once the ghost—a blue shadow on a backstage wall, with the recorded voice of John Gielgud speaking its commands—has handed on to him the secret of the death that will scandalize Denmark, he is suddenly a small boy who knows all the truths of the dark. With a leap and a smile and an energy born of gloating, he almost dances out his joy at the wild, wicked joke of life. He has a bond now with the father he loved, and it produces something more than hate: it produces humor.

The art of Holywood has never especially appealed to Burton. He says he much prefers the stage. But there is money in it, huge quantities, in the eyes of a lad brought up in poverty. The true stature of his talents do not seem to come through in *Hamlet* on film. Actually the play was filmed in the New York theatre and distributed for showing simultaneously in some 1,200 cities in the United States, which made it possible for many thousands to see his Hamlet who would not otherwise have done so. Once one adjusted to the fact that it was not a movie, but simply a filming of a stage performance, it could, and did, prove most moving.

And so through three and a half centuries, from Burbage to Burton one views the notable Hamlets of the theatre. Styles vary, stages vary, costumes vary, yet audience appeal remains ever strong. The creator of this unique play could surely have had no conception of its success.

Whenever an actor properly endowed for the role appears, people will flock to acclaim him. Mid-twentieth century bears due witness to this. It is difficult to imagine a time when one concludes, "We have seen the last of the Hamlets."

XVIII

A PLENTIFUL LACK OF WIT

HAMLET, PERHAPS MORE than any play in the dramatic repertory, has fared badly and suffered atrociously at the hands of mortal men and women. Text, staging, costuming have been tampered with and "improved" in the name of sound learning, and there is scarcely a creature crawling between heaven and earth who has not felt specially appointed to fret and play upon the role. By wisdom and genius the strength and stature of the play have been preserved for us; the unaccountable tastes of a bygone age survive in the records, for our laughter.

In this concluding chapter, whose title has been chosen from some of Hamlet's ironic words addressed to Polonius, are recalled some of the more droll and lighter elements that have marked the path of the play, particularly during the nineteenth century.

From the late Garrick period to the early Booth, it was necessary for managers to follow a performance of tragedy with a farce, a program dictated by audience demands. Hamlet himself was seldom compelled to don grimacing motley, but other players did so. Playbills of *Hamlet* reveal a certain partiality for personalities: *Barney Brallagan; or Meet Me by Moonlight* (1831), *Betsy Baker; or Too Attentive by Half* (1866). There is a suggestion of the seven ages of man in the sequence of: *Belles Have at Ye All; or More Flirts than One* (1815); *Three Weeks after Marriage; or What we must all come to* (1821), *Spring and Autumn; or The Bride at Fifty.*

This is no idle dreaming upon fiction. Solemn performances of *Hamlet* had their concluding farces and often the most appallingly inappropriate

Count Johannes (George Jones) as Hamlet, 1810-1879

Stephen Kemble in 1794

music conceivable. There was even a falling off in nineteenth-century taste. Turning from Mozart, Rossini, Auber and others, orchestras displayed a preference for waltzes, marches, patrols, potpourris, and the latest popular tunes. Imagine *Hamlet* to the accompaniment of "The Blue Danube"!

But the twentieth century has had its way. Modern-dress versions at least proved to the general satisfaction that the play was hard to spoil. In some scenes and at certain moments it was amazingly vital. Nevertheless, Hamlet at the grave of Ophelia garbed in knickerbockers and a traveling cap was not altogether convincing.

In the winter of 1878 a gentleman who styled himself Count Johannes appeared as Hamlet in New York. A victim of a practical joke in his early professional career, George Jones had assumed a title. And now, approaching seventy, he gave a performance that so caught the fancy of the gay blades of the town that they crowded nightly into the theatre for their merciless pleasure. Scarcely a line failed to provoke sallies of wit. There was general hubbub until the final curtain. Showers of "gifts" for the pitiful actor fell upon the stage. Neither imprecations hurled against the audience nor appeals for fair play availed to alter their predetermined conduct.

The Count thought to escape the violence of New York by retreating several miles up the Hudson River to Nyack, where in more pastoral village calm he took the precaution of defending his stage with a huge net. His enthusiastic followers, nothing daunted, attended in a body. Though the net saved Hamlet's clothes, it did not charge the theatre with an atmosphere that was pastoral. The "run" had come to an end. Another Hamlet, James Owen O'Connor, in emulation of the success of the luckless Count, made use of a net, deliberately calculating the effect on the box-office.

Grotesque Hamlets there have been in full measure, though we may, with a reasonable kindness, assume that faulty artistry in illustration depicted them not altogether in their true colors. We are compelled to admit that Stephen Kemble was fat. As for the ladies, the weight of evidence is crushing. Let it suffice to record that Elsie Kearns was once a Hamlet, and Oliph Webb another.

Though since Shakespeare's time male Juliets have been rare, the nineteenth century called forth this rich effusion of female Hamlets. The fashion seems to have been started by Mrs. Siddons, gathered momentum

Sarah Bernhardt as Hamlet

Sarah Bernhardt as Hamlet at Adelphi Theatre, London

CHARLOTTE CRAMPTON as HAMLET.

Charlotte Crampton
Glass of fashion and mold of form

Eliza Warren as Hamlet
Sweet bells out of 'tune

toward the appearance of Charlotte Cushman, and with the advent of the 1850's flowered to a seemingly endless line of princesses of Denmark. There are on record dozens of actresses who played the part, none of them to any appreciable satisfaction for their audiences. To the two great actresses whose names have been mentioned one must add that of Sarah Bernhardt.

The "divine" Sarah, idol of the French stage and world-renowned through her many tours, was more than fifty years of age when she essayed to appear as Hamlet. With a French version of the play in Paris, where she could do no wrong, she was greeted with enthusiasm; not so in London and New York. Is it to the discredit of one London reviewer that he never found a Hamlet less fatiguing? This same reviewer, we hasten to add, spoke disparagingly of Booth. He liked Mme. Bernardt's scenes with Polonius and particularly praised the "business" of the speech to the players being delivered from the miniature stage—an actor addressing his audience. The Athenaeum of June 17, 1899, gives us: "Where everything is necessarily wrong, nothing can be right."

Some of our female Hamlets made frequent appearances over a period of years. Mme. Barnhardt's experiment was short-lived. Her Hamlet was seen in New York in the autumn of 1899. William Winter wrote of her as "looking exactly like what she was, a thin, elderly woman, somewhat disguised" and that her Hamlet "died standing, and his reeling body was caught by Horatio; and subsequently it was borne away—to the general relief—upon huge shields."

When Max Beerbohm succeeded Shaw as dramatic critic of *The Saturday Review,* he confessed to having no fondness for the theatre. He certainly gave way to no fondness for the interpretation of Sarah Bernhardt in his criticism designated, "Hamlet, Princess of Denmark":

> I cannot, on my heart, take Sarah's Hamlet seriously. I cannot even imagine anyone capable of more than a hollow pretense of taking it seriously. However, the truly great are apt, in matters concerning themselves, to lose that sense of fitness which is usually called a sense of humor, and I did not notice that Sarah was once hindered in her performance by any irresistible desire to burst out laughing. Her solemnity was politely fostered by the Adelphi audience. From first to last no one smiled. One laugh in that dangerous atmosphere, and the whole structure of polite solemnity would have toppled down, burying beneath its ruins the national reputation for good manners.

Sarah ought not to have supposed that Hamlet's weakness set him in any possible relation to her own feminine mind and body. Her friends ought to have restrained her. The native critics ought not to have encouraged her. The custom-house officials at Charing Cross ought to have confiscated her sable doublet and hose. I, lover of her incomparable art, am even more distressed than amused when I think of her aberration at the Adelphi. . . Her perfect self-possession was one of the most remarkable elements in the evening's comedy, but one could not help being genuinely impressed by her dignity.

(Knopf 1930): *Around Theatres*

BIBLIOGRAPHY

ALGER, W. R., *The Life of Edwin Forrest,* (Philadelphia 1877).

ANONYMOUS, *The Actor, or a Treatise on the Art of Playing,* (London 1755).

ARCHER, WILLIAM, *Henry Irving, Actor and Manager,* (London 1883); *Macready,* (London 1890); *The Fashionable Tragedian,* (unsigned criticism), (London 1878).

ARCHER, WILLIAM, and LOWE, ROBERT W., *Dramatic Essays by John Forster, George Henry Lewes,* (London 1896); *Dramatic Essays — William Hazlitt,* (London 1895).

BARRETT, LAWRENCE, *Edwin Forrest,* (James R. Osgood 1881).

BARRYMORE, JOHN, *Confessions of an Actor,* (Bobbs-Merril 1926).

BEERBOHM, MAX, *Around Theatres* (Knopf 1930).

BOADEN, JAMES, *Memoirs of the Life of John Philip Kemble Esq.,* (London 1825).

BRERETON, AUSTIN, *Shakespearean Scenes and Characters,* (London 1886); *Some Famous Hamlets from Burbage to Fechter,* (London 1884).

BROWN, JOHN MASON, *Two on the Aisle,* (W.W. Norton 1938).

BROWN, JOHN MASON, and MOSES, MONTROSE J., *The American Theatre as Seen by Its Critics,* (W. W. Norton 1934).

CHALMERS, ALEXANDER, *Complete Works of Shakespeare,* (2 vols. Constable, London, 1921).

CIBBER, COLLEY, *Apology for His Life,* (London 1740).

CLAPP, HENRY AUSTIN, *Reminiscences of a Dramatic Critic,* (New York 1880).

CLARKE, ASIA BOOTH, *The Elder and the Younger Booth,* (James R. Osgood 1882).

COLLIER, J. PAYNE, *Memoirs of Edward Alleyn, Founder of Dulwich College,* (London 1841); *Memoirs of the Principal Actors in the Plays of Shakespeare,* (London 1846).

CONGDON, CHARLES T., *Reminiscences of a Journalist,* (New York 1880).

COOK, DUTTON, *Hours with the Players,* (London 1883).

COPELAND, CHARLES TOWNSEND, *Edwin Booth,* (Boston 1901).

DAVIES, THOMAS, *Dramatic Miscellanies,* (London 1784).

DORAN, DR. JOHN, *Annals of the English Stage from Thomas Betterton to Edmund Kean,* (Their Majesties' Servants — People's Edition, London, 1885).

DOWNES, JOHN, *Roscius Angelicanus or an Historical Review of the Stage,* (London 1708).

FIELD, KATE, *Charles A. Fechter,* (Boston 1882).

FORBES-ROBERTSON, SIR JOHNSTON, *A Player Under Three Reigns* (Little, Brown & Co. 1925).

GRAY, CHARLES HAROLD NEWCOMB, *Edmund Kean,* (Columbia University Press 1933).

LEWES, GEORGE HENRY, *On Actors and the Art of Acting,* (London 1875).

LOCKRIDGE, RICHARD, *Darling of Misfortune — Edwin Booth,* (Century Company 1932).

LOWE, ROBERT W., *Thomas Betterton,* (London 1891).

MARTIN, SIR THEODORE, *Monographs,* (Murray, London,1906).

Monthly Miscellany, (London 1814).

MURPHY, ARTHUR, *The Life of David Garrick,* (London 1801).

ODELL, GEORGE C. D.,*Shakespeare from Betterton to Irving,* (2 vols. Constable, London, 1921).

POLLOCK, SIR FREDERICK, *Reminiscences of the Life of William Charles Macready.*

PROCTOR, B. W. *The Life of Edmund Kean,* (London 1835).

ROBINS, EDWARD, *Twelve Great Actors,* (New York 1900).

RUSSELL, EDWARD R., *Irving as Hamlet,* (London 1875).

SALVINI, TOMMASO, *Leaves from the Autobiography of Tommaso Salvini* (London, 1893).

Stage, The, (London 1814 and 1815).

STRANG, LEWIS C., *Famous Actors of the Day in America,* (Second Series), (L. C. Page & Co. 1902).

Theatre, The; or Dramatic and Literary Mirror, (Vols. 1 & 2, London 1819).

Theatrical Inquisitor, and Monthly Mirror, (Vol. 6, London 1815).

Theatrical Review, The (London 1758 and 1763).

WILLIAMS, JOHN AMBROSE, *Memoirs of John Philip Kemble,* (London 1817).

WINTER, WILLIAM, *Shakespeare on the Stage,* (Moffat, Yard & Co. 1911); *The Life of Edwin Booth,* (London 1893).

BURBAGE · BETTERTON ·
FORREST · MACREADY ·
SALVINI·FORBES-ROBER
BARRYMORE · GIELGU

ARRICK · KEMBLE · KEAN

OOTH · FECHTER · IRVING

ON-SOTHERN·HAMPDEN

EVANS · BURTON